Excerpts from
SATAN'S MUSIC EXPO[SED]

Satan, who has been trying to get a toehold i[n] [the evan-]
gelical church, has found a wide open back doo[r] [and is being]
blindly but enthusiastically welcomed by the m[any.]

* * *

We are becoming so preoccupied with the *"let's be contemporary"* theme
that we seem blithely unaware that the world, like a gigantic whirlpool, has
sucked us into its orbit and is dragging us steadily down to disaster.

Chapter 2

* * *

Many secular pop stars claim the salvation experience. They are cashing in
on our gullibility by traveling about the country appearing at youth meetings
and Christian television programs while at the same time happily riding the
night club circuit.

Chapter 3

* * *

A missionary took back to Africa with him records of semi-classical music
and acid rock. He played both to members of the local tribe. The results
were extremely surprising!

Chapter 6

* * *

Today Rock-n-roll is being heard in Christian homes across the land. By
merely adding religious words it also is suddenly transformed into the *"new"*
church music.

Chapter 8

* * *

Rock music is a pollutant every bit as deadly as pornography. Rock, with its
almost total emphasis on the beat, bypasses the mind and works directly
on the body. The Beatles admitted, *"Our music is capable of causing emotional instability, disorganized behavior, rebellion and even revolution."*

Chapter 9

* * *

Some well-known Christian song writers are including the sensual rock tunes
in their Cantatas, musicals and song books. The words of much of their music
are vague at best and the music imitates the world.

Chapter 15

* * *

The statement, *"You'll never reach unsaved young people with traditional
church music"* is not only false and immature, but limits the power of God!

Chapter 16

* * *

**All this and *much more* you will find in the chapters of this exciting and
revealing book that provides you with new information that will make *Satan's
Music Exposed!***

IMPORTANT! PLEASE READ!

In this book, **SATAN'S MUSIC EXPOSED,** it has been necessary to name specific song titles or music artists in order to convey the type of music we find objectionable.

In our opinion, the music we identify is worldly and does not promote the cause of Christ.

Nothing in this book should be construed as to undermining those believers whose music opinions differ from us. Nor do we doubt their dedicated desire to win souls to Christ.

Our disagreement is not with them, but with some of their music which we believe is not in harmony with the deeper Christian life.

Nothing in this book is to be construed as labeling or accusing any musical group, song or record as being Satanic. Just as Christ in Matthew 16:23 said to Peter, *"Get thee behind me, Satan . . . ,"* it is the author's opinion that sincere believers sometimes unknowingly advance Satan's work. This alone is the theme of this book.

Salem Kirban

SATAN'S MUSIC EXPOSED

by Lowell Hart

Photo Commentary by
Salem Kirban

Published by SALEM KIRBAN, Inc., Mason's Mill Road, Huntingdon Valley, Pennsylvania 19006. Copyright© 1980 by Salem Kirban. Printed in the United States of America. All rights reserved, including the right to reproduce this book or portions thereof in any form.

Library of Congress Catalog Card No. 80-83387
ISBN 0-912582-35-9

ACKNOWLEDGEMENTS

To **Dr. Gary G. Cohen,** President of Clearwater Christian College, Clearwater, Florida, who carefully checked the final manuscript.

To **Doreen Frick,** who devoted many hours proofreading the text.

To **Estelle Bair Composition,** for excellent craftsmanship in setting the type.

To **Walter W. Slotilock,** Chapel Hill Litho, for negatives.

To **Koechel Designs,** for an excellent cover design.

CONTENTS

Foreword

Here is a much needed book on a very misunderstood subject—what is Christian music?

Some would have us believe that all music is a-moral and that it is only the words that make it Christian or not. I beg to differ with this philosophy! This book does much to prove that music in itself is a language which can capture and control the very thoughts and actions of an individual, a crowd, or a nation. It is the fountainhead for good or for evil! As one must be discerning in the device of their friends and their food for a happy and healthy life . . . so we must be careful and prayerful in the music we chose to listen to or sing.

With the apostle Paul I would encourage each one to *"Let the Word of Christ dwell in you richly in all wisdom; teaching and admonishing one another in Psalms and hymns and spiritual songs, singing with grace in your hearts to the Lord and whatsoever you do in word or deed, do all in the name of the Lord Jesus, giving thanks to God and the Father by Him."* (Colossians 3:16,17)

'Sing"cerely,

Dr. Alfred B. Smith
Melody Manor
Montrose, PA 18801

Dr. Alfred B. Smith is the Compiler and Editor of **LIVING HYMNS** hymnbook. He is also the author of many familiar hymns and choruses including the chorus, *"For God So Loved The World."*

WHY I WROTE THIS BOOK

Many years ago, as a then young non-Christian dance band musician, I enjoyed playing in ballrooms and night clubs. If anyone had suggested to me then that this same music would some day be heard in evangelical churches as the *"now"* sound, I would have regarded their suggestion as the best joke of the day.

Today we are hearing this sound. But it is no joke! It is a pitiful paradox. Songs like *"Amazing Grace," "O Happy Day"* and *"The Lord's Prayer"* have been played on rock stations. Rock, jazz and blues are being heard in the church, and though many Christians are questioning the trend, few are speaking out against it.

Many Christian young people think it is just about the best thing that has ever come along. Parents are confused, and many Christian leaders and pastors admit they do not know enough about music to make a decision when questions do arise. To add to the confusion, many well-known Christian musicians who were formerly traditionalists are now pushing contemporary sounds.

You may be puzzled, amused or even a bit angered at the title of this book. Your reaction might be, *"Who does he think he is, making such a gross condemnation of Christian music?"*

It is my hope that by the time you have finished the last chapter you will see why I believe **SATAN'S MUSIC EXPOSED** correctly describes the modern trend in church music! Whether you are a teen or a parent my prayer is that you will be helped in your evaluation of contemporary music.

Three Hills, Alberta   Lowell Hart
Canada / September, 1980

1

HAMBURGERS, FRENCH FRIES, AND CHRISTIAN MUSIC

Like the hamburger-French fry diet of today (that has re-placed the nutritious foods of grandfather's day) the teen-ager's fare of today's Christian music, with its frothy, candy-coated content, has been substituted for the solid meat of Luther, Wesley, Watts, and Sankey.

* * *

Satan, who has been trying to get a toehold in the front door of the evangelical church, has found a wide open back door through which he has been blindly but enthu-siastically welcomed by the medium of music.

* * *

Whatever these two songbooks are trying to accomplish, it is not the praise of God and the edification of believers!

* * *

Today there is often little difference between the teens' Top 40 music and what the youth choir sings on Sunday evenings.

1

HAMBURGERS, FRENCH FRIES, AND CHRISTIAN MUSIC

**Holy
Temple
Rock**

On my desk is a cartoon clipped from a now forgotten magazine of many issues back. It shows the inside of a beautiful and stately church. On the platform are three bushy young musicians flailing away at their electrically amplified instruments. In the congregation sits a very confused middle-aged couple. The man turns to his wife and says,

> This is not my idea of 'The Lord is in His Holy Temple, Let All the Earth Keep Silent Before Him.'

I smiled when I first saw it. Yet it did not take long to see that the cartoonist had hit on an area that is not at all amusing. Similar groups of various sizes and sounds are being heard all over the country spreading the *"sounds of the now generation."* They may be called <u>The New Folk</u>, <u>The Armageddon Experience</u>, <u>The Power and Light Company</u>, <u>The Second</u>

Chapter of Acts, New Hope, or Love Song. They are made up of young people who bubble with zeal and enthusiasm as they sing and play their way into the traditional worship services of the church. Their music throbs, jumps, swings. It is dreamy and sentimental, bright and bouncy. It is rock. It is blues. It is folk. It is Top Forty.

And it is deadly!

Candy Coated Music

Today in many places the contemporary sound has all but replaced the older hymns and gospel songs that once were sung as an expression of worship and praise and that brought comfort and inspiration to countless congregations. Like the hamburger-French fry diet of today (that has replaced the nutritious foods of grandfather's day) the teen-agers' fare of today's Christian music, with its frothy, candy-coated content, has been substituted for the solid meat of Luther, Wesley, Watts, and Sankey. In search of something that will reach turned-off youth, many have incorporated the sweet but empty sounds of the world into Christian music in hopes of spreading the good news. Unfortunately, this unholy alliance of pop music with church music is leading many young people into distorted concepts and false impressions of the Christian life. The watered-down theology found in many of the new songs accompanied by rock sounds says in effect: *"Christianity isn't so bad after all. It's not much different from your life-style. Just grab hold of Jesus and join us."*

Satan Enters The Back Door

Satan, who has been trying to get a toehold in the front door of the evangelical church, has found a wide open back door through which he has been blindly but enthusiastically welcomed by the medium of music.

The new music did not just suddenly drop from nowhere into the church. The downward slide has been subtly in process for some time. A generation ago the music of the church could rarely be mistaken for pop music. There was a difference, and everyone recognized it. Over a period of years there has been a gradual moving away from *"psalms and hymns and spiritual songs"* until today, when there is often little difference between the teens' Top 40 music and what the youth choir sings on Sunday evenings!

The Subtle Drift

I first began to notice this drift a few years ago when, as a member of a Christian record club, I began having to send more and more records back because the music was becoming more like what I had played in my dance band days, and the lyrics were becoming more sentimental than scriptural.

Today all the barriers are down. Available now for church choirs are such choice selections as Daniel Jazz, Jonahman Jazz, The Lord's Thing, Joseph and the Amazing Technicolor Dreamcoat, Messiah A La Moog, and Electric Church. Or you may select from a song series, Hymns Hot and Carols Cool—all arranged with the beat and bounce of rock and jazz. These are published not by some unknown off-beat music company, but by some of the largest and most reputable Christian publishing houses in the United States!

Sacrilegious Contents

Consider The Genesis Songbook (Agape 1974), a songbook for youth. It is *"dedicated to the bald as well as the short and long hairs; young and old, Christians and pagans and even sinners"* (underline mine). In it are songs by folk-rock star Bob Dylan, John Lennon and Paul McCartney of the Beatles, and pop song writer Paul Simon, among others. It is a mixture of pop and folk tunes, semi-religious songs, with only a sprinkling of traditional hymns and choruses. Some are antiscriptural as in Lord of the Dance: *"I danced on a Friday when the sky turned black. It's hard to dance with the devil on your back."* One is a sarcastic slam against evangelical Christianity: from Mrs. Robinson, *"And here's to you, Mrs. Robinson, Jesus loves you more than you will know (wo, wo, wo). God bless you, Mrs. Robinson, heaven holds a place for those who pray (hey, hey, hey)."* Number 29 in the book is a poem by Paul Simon, Blessed. It is blasphemy.

> . . . Blessed are the stained glass.
>   Window pane glass.
>   Blessed is the church service
>   Makes me nervous.
>   Blessed are the penny rookers;
>   Cheap hookers, groovy lookers.
>   O Lord, why have you forsaken me?
>   I have tended my own garden
>   much too long.

A collection of 74 songs is published in the **Genesis** songbook. The book is dedicated to ". . . *Christians and Pagans and even sinners!*" It includes music by John Lennon of the Beatles (Imagine) and Paul Simon (Ms. Robinson). A follow-up songbook titled **Exodus** includes "*The Holy Spirit and Elmer's Glue.*" Both are published by a well-known hymn book publishing company.

The Genesis Songbook is being sold in Christian book stores (and not under the counter), at Bible camps, and can be found in Christian homes. In spite of the above blasphemous selections, The Genesis Songbook must have been a big seller. It was followed three years later with—as you might guess—The Exodus Songbook.

Listen To The Words

Like its predecessor, The Exodus Songbook is a collection of pop and folk songs with a handful of familiar gospel songs to make it fit the *"religious"* category. From the introduction about its contents: *"Some [songs] are sacred, some profane, some unknown . . ."* Here is a sampling:

Alfie. From the Paramount picture, Alfie:

> *"As sure as I believe there's a heaven above, Alfie, I know there's something much more, something even non-believers can believe in. I believe in love, Alfie."*

Kodachrome. *"When I think back on all the crap I learned in high school, it's a wonder I can think at all . . ."*

It Ain't Necessarily So. *". . . oh, I takes dat gospel whenever it's possible. But wid' a grain of salt . . ."*

Sing You Sinners. From the MGM film, I'll Cry Tomorrow: *"Brothers and sisters my sermon today is pa-doop-poop-poop and vo deo do and sing your troubles away."* (This is a sermon?)

The Holy Spirit and Elmer's Glue. *"We're bound to each other whatever we do by the Holy Spirit and Elmer's glue."*

American Pie, song number 58, matches Paul Simon's Blessed in its blasphemy:

> ". . . and not a word was spoken, the church bells were broken, and the three men I admire the most, the Father, Son and Holy Ghost, they caught the last train for the coast."

Marxist, anti-Christian propaganda? No. Printed in America in the name of Christianity. Whatever these two songbooks are trying to accomplish, it is not the praise of God and the edification of believers!

While not all contemporary music publications may be as extreme as the Genesis and Exodus songbooks, they do point to a deterioration that would have been unimagined less than a generation ago.

2

CONFORMING TO THE WORLD

Our entire Christian life-style has been eroding, and with it the music! During one song, the trumpet player of the Salvation Army group called The Hallelujah Sound, took off on a *"hot ride."* His hips swung back and forth as he played. Before the evening was over the entire audience (but one) was swinging and swaying.

* * *

We are becoming so preoccupied with the *"let's be contemporary"* theme that we seem blithely unaware that the world, like a gigantic whirlpool, has sucked us into its orbit and is dragging us steadily down to disaster.

* * *

The setting up of their own standards (*"you'll never reach young people unless . . ."* etc.) is not unusual for those who are trying to interest young people in the gospel with the Madison Avenue approach. Sincere as they may be, those who use these methods are substituting human philosophy and effort for simple obedience to God's Word.

* * *

It is not the godly men who are leading the new music trend. It is the *"unprincipled,"* the carnally-minded . . .

2

CONFORMING TO THE WORLD

**Diet
From A
Garbage
Can**

Because I am daily involved with young people as well as with music, I try to keep up on current musical trends. Styles change frequently and it is difficult to know what is "in" almost from one month to the next. So I do a lot of listening to contemporary music. Sometimes it is enjoyable. Very often it is not. It is like trying to get my meals from the contents of a garbage can—not very appetizing. As a Christian I don't feel comfortable listening to certain types of music which are popular with many Christian young people today. It isn't a matter of a generation gap. Nor is it merely a matter of personal taste. Our entire Christian life-style has been eroding, and with it the music!

Paul wrote to Timothy (2 Timothy 4:2-4 NASV):

*Preach the word; be ready in season
and out of season; reprove, rebuke,
exhort, with great patience and in-
struction. For the time will come
when they will not endure sound doctrine; but wanting to have their ears
tickled, they will accumulate for
themselves teachers in accordance
to their own desires; and will turn
away their ears from the truth, and
will turn aside to myths.*

What we are seeing today in the church is
a manifestation of these words.

**My
First
Encounter**

One of my first experiences with the Now
Sound music came a few years ago when
a Christian rock group, representing a
small Christian college, came to town to
present a *"contemporary sacred concert"*
in the local high school gymnasium. It was
typical of the scores of similar groups that
were springing up all over the country in
colleges and church youth groups. The
phenomenon of *"Christian"* rock was then
just getting a start. I had never heard one
of these groups live and thought it might
be interesting, though I really didn't know
what to expect. I changed into my usual
concert-going attire and drove across
town to the school. The sign over the door
read *"couples - $1.25, singles - 75¢."* I
wasn't sure if it was going to be a dance
or a concert. But I bought my ticket and
went in anyway.

**Initiating
The
World**

The concert was scheduled for 8:00. By
8:20, and with no sign of the performers,
the audience began to get a little restless

Larry Norman
HIS LATEST ALBUM
IN ANOTHER LAND

Aerosmith fans were blown away. Van Halen people had their socks rocked off. Kiss groupies were appalled and shocked. Ted Nugent devotees called it 'ruder than rude'.

We had heard rumours that the Larry Norman Band played hard rock 'n' roll.

Musical juice cranked up, the band cooked into "Why Should the Devil Have All the Good Music", Norman boiling out like an unwatched pot. Steaming into "Let The Tape Keep Rollin'" brought the evening to a sizzling climax.

Screaming, wild applause and an audience determined to have an encore brought back the Band for "I Wish We'd All Been Ready", which broke into a hard, apocalyptic jam with Norman screaming "Why? Don't be left behind!" He walked off while the band jammed on.

The rock was rolling, and it was hard enough for anybody. The devil doesn't have all the good music. He's got nothing on the Larry Norman Band.

"The devil will try to steal anything Christians leave lying around," Norman insists. Is rock music satanic? Norman insists it comes from the church. "Remember when we brought all those people over from Africa to help out for the summer?" He starts a black spiritual, slow and restrained, "If I got my ticket, Lord, can I ride?" He picks it up. A little nastier, gravellier, hotter and pretty soon we've got rock 'n' roll. "Now you pick a tune" he says. Someone yells "Swing low, Sweet chariot" "Good", he replies "that's close enough to rock 'n' roll." "I look over Jordan and what do I see?" Norman sings, "A pick-up truck full o' white folks comin' after me." Adding a few doe, doe's it sounds like the fifties. Norman did "Nightmare", a song about "the history of civilization up until a couple days ago." People won't stop clapping. "What's the name of that disease?" he asks. "If God is My Father" slides into "The Outlaw".

Above are portions of a news article on the **Larry Norman Band** when in concert in Vancouver, British Columbia. The article states that Larry Norman is the *"father of Jesus rock."* A full page news report appeared in Firewind . . . a music oriented publication.

and noisy. I noticed a young fellow of about 19 or 20 dressed in a white T-shirt and faded jeans, whom I supposed to be the janitor, still setting up chairs in the back. I was more than surprised when the "janitor" took a running leap on to the stage and introduced himself as the leader of the group. He was then joined by the other members who were all about his age and dressed in the same faded jean T-shirt ensemble.

This was somewhat different from the sharp red and white uniforms of high school days and later the purple and gold of the University of Washington band I had worn. But at least the jeans were faded the same color. That was a uniform of sorts. I looked around at the predominantly teen-age audience. They were dressed the same as the performers. My suit and tie looked decidedly out of place. I was beginning to feel a bit uncomfortable.

As the leader began his introductions, telling everyone how glad they were to be there and that the only reason for their coming was to glorify God, my mind began to wander. I thought of how nice it would be if, instead of following the world in fashions and music, Christians would set the standards . . .

Ear Splitting Sounds

Before I could finish my reflections, the concert began. The first chord exploded over the audience ricochetting off the walls in an ear-splitting roar. We were off! The group had two levels—loud and louder! The young audience clapped along, talked among themselves, and they were obviously enjoying it. My ears hurt. What few words they were singing that could be heard over the loud accompaniment didn't seem to relate in any way to the music. The lyrics were about God, but they didn't go with the earthly, sensuous style of the ensemble's delivery. I wasn't enjoying it very much.

But I had paid my 75¢ and was determined to get my money's worth. It wasn't that the group did not show sincerity. They were trying hard to relate to their listeners. But being sincere was not enough to put the concern on any higher plane spiritually. They were relating all right. But on the wrong level.

I left the gymnasium that night with my ears ringing, my senses dulled, and depressed about the whole thing. It wasn't that I had missed the point. The concert was obviously aimed at teens. I wondered, though, does God have one standard for adults and another for young people?

Even The Salvation Army . . .

Later that same year another contemporary group came to town. They called themselves The Hallelujah Sound, representing the Salvation Army. The only Salvation Army groups I had known were the excellent brass bands that played stirring arrangements of hymns and concert pieces. This one was different. They were an ensemble of six, and younger than most of the standard groups. In place of the traditional brass were two electric guitars, electric organ, drums, and alto sax. The only brass instrument was one trumpet. The audience was about equally divided between youth and adult. This time, at least, I didn't feel quite so out of place.

The spokesman for the group announced that the concert would be in two parts—the first, the more formal and traditional,—and the second, informal and contemporary, and that they *"just wanted to praise the Lord."* With that the concert began. The first chord exploded over the audience, bouncing off the walls. . . . The sound was familiar. I wondered if all the new groups opened their concerts this way.

Old Rugged Cross Rock Version

Some of the traditional hymns turned out to be not so traditional. Or at least the music wasn't. Hearing a rock version of *"The Old Rugged Cross"* is a memorable experience! During intermission they exchanged their black and red uniforms for casual street clothes. This was to be the informal part. It was.

During one song the trumpet player took off on a *"hot ride,"* hips swinging back and forth as he played. What this had to do with the gospel song he was playing, I didn't know. Before the evening was over the entire audience (all but one!) was swinging and swaying to the glorious beat. If you have never watched a group of middle-aged people swaying back and forth in the pews and clapping their hands to the music, you've missed something.

This was the Salvation Army? What

Salvation Army Trades Anthems for Rock Music

It's unlikely that long-haired, modly dressed members of the Salvation Army will soon be playing the Beatles' "Help" instead of "The Old Rugged Cross" on street corners across the land.

But the Army, that long-time bastion of brass instrumentalists playing standard hymns, is experimenting with rock music. And while the idea doesn't sound bad to some Salvationists, it strikes a jarring note among many in the organization, where short, neatly trimmed hair is the general rule.

In an effort to spread its message of evangelical Christianity to young people this summer, the Army's Eastern Territory sponsored a tour by a hard-playing, 13-member, teen - age rock group called, appropriately enough, "The Salvation Army Band."

Though most of the Army's 1,300 units in the country still play traditional music, the Salvationists have also recently supported rock bands in the Midwest and Nova Scotia.

Cutback on Street Bands

The band's tour comes at a time when the Army has been cutting back on the number of its street units and sometimes relying on cassette tape players for the music. In New York City, for example, bands can only be heard in the Times Square area and then only rarely.

The cutback was caused partly by the fear of street crime and partly because people are no longer attracted as much by brass music, explained Capt. Carl L. Schoch, New York Divisional Youth Secretary.

However, the captain said, "We still go out at Christmas because people expect it of us."

can be interpreted by committed Christians.

In the group' Jesus is the one are calling on when they sing if you can, I'm l And I do appr bein' 'round." A Sweat and Tears "Bless the Child members explai words "them th mean "the more gether with Chri peace and joy return."

This summer's ered major Eas Each bandsman educational scho room and board, the 13 are not S but are friends of musicians and b evangelistic faiths the Army's.

Major Kelly is with the Band' plans to establish nent section in devoted to youth

"It's not the typ but the saving of s important," he sai

At Star Lake, the of most of the old tionists was the natured politeness who are accustome erating drunken heck

"I suppose it's ni just can't relate to Mrs. Janet K. Sp housewife and Army

Many younger Sa ists don't appreciat music either, Major said. "Just look at who were listening weren't clapping alon didn't know what t he said.

And Mr. Steadman said the Army's exper with rock wouldn't la: "You can't marc rock," he said.

60,000 teen-agers dig new hard-rock religion

New York — It's on the wild side, sponsors admit. But the teen-agers dig it. And they're snapping it up and calling for more.

"You don't catch fish with cement," says Pastor Harold M.S. Richards Jr., of Glendale, Calif., director of the broadcasting arm of the Seventh-day Adventist Church, and in charge of the new program.

It's called "The Way Out." It enlists the way-out styles of youngsters — their hard rock sounds, their psychedelic colors and their monosyllabic hip lingo — to hook them on the truths of Jesus instead of drugs, astrology, vibrations and incense.

He "knows where it's at . . . about love and peace and digging life and each other," says one brochure. "He was on a genuine love trip without the use of artificial stimulants or religious coverups."

Five-month test

The program, developed by the Voice of Prophecy, the Adventists' 40-year-old broadcasting operation, was spot tested from February to June on eight of about 40 top rock'n roll stations in the country and drew heavy response.

"Really with it," wrote one teen-ager, among more than 60,000 responding. Other comments: "Far out and fabulous." "You really know how to tell it like it is." "Neat and groovy." "It really stuck in my thoughts." "Wow!"

In mid-summer, the pro-

gram started expanding to a nationwide basis. "We want to blanket North America with it," said a spokesman, Herbert Ford. It relies on breezy messages, aired on paid time of leading rock-music stations, offering free mailed items, produced in the same hip fashion.

Rock stations used

These stations have the ear of 90 percent of teen-agers who listen to radio, a survey showed. "This made us fully aware that we would be talking to thin air unless we used rock-and-roll stations to carry our appeal," Pastor Richards said.

But the stations wouldn't accept conventional religious advertising, he noted, insisting that it be "short and sound like us." To meet the requirements of those particular stations, the messages are kept in snappy, hip language, against backgrounds of mod music. The same mood, garish layouts and cool talk prevails in the literature offered free to listeners.

"No bread," the mailed pieces note, listing other materials available gratis on various subjects aggravating youth — astrology, the occult, parents, drugs, homosexuality, sex and veneral disease.

The initial mailings are issues of "Way Out" magazine, including numbers introducing Jesus, "The Man from Way Out," and his work, the "Way Out Trip."

"Jesus had always being in helping a br hurting inside, cifully decorat knew people around heavy heads, and he ate them . . . that.

"No matt times a br Jesus is right him out of . . . He libera a life . . . Bi is based on not on ego power, violen out. . ."

Staff lead church and groups, Crusade and I have asked fi to use in th local congreg soring the I local rock st

After the

One "hang puts the que pens after th poses the q young gene overtur lishment, w will come ou

"Blowing groovy, but be able to p to create world' . . . scene is on What if beh ing, love-ma dream wor are on

The Salvation Army and the Seventh-Day Adventists' *Voice of Prophecy* have used religious Rock to "attract" followers.

No Different From The World

would General Booth have thought?

Not many months later a third group was in the area. I wasn't sure I wanted to hear them but decided at the last minute that I should go. Maybe it would be different from the others. It was, in a way. In contrast to the other two, they didn't major in volume. Their music was more subdued and refined. Yet it was there, subtly but unmistakably, the throbbing beat that characterized the others. Their smooth blues-folk style renditions of hymns and newer gospel songs crooned into hand mikes and delivered with polish and split-second timing was pure night club. The singers, like those of the first two groups, were sincerely trying to get a message across. But again the medium contradicted the message.

In the few years that have gone by since the initial shock of hearing "Christian" music that is essentially the same as I had played in ball rooms, I have attended other performances of contemporary groups, have listened to dozens of the latest contemporary recordings, and have examined many of the newest songs and choral arrangements. There has been little change. The trend continues, always closer and closer to the world.

So thoroughly entrenched in contemporary Christian society is the "now sound" that to suggest a return to some of the more traditional hymns and old favorites is often to be met with "get off your horse and buggy, man," shakes of the head, or a lecture on how the only way to reach today's generation is with music they understand. It's frustrating—like rowing upstream in a leaky boat using only a soup ladle as a paddle, trying to keep from being swept over the falls.

A Vague Message

This downward trend is no mere passing phenomenon. Observes Dave Hendricks, manager of Christian radio station WBYO, in reviewing his 25 years in radio,

"We seem to be getting more and more pseudo-religious songs whose message is vague at best. . . . We find it necessary to tighten reins all the time as much of the music sounds more and more like the world."[1]

We are becoming so preoccupied with the *"let's be contemporary"* theme that we seem blithely unaware that the world, like a gigantic whirlpool, has sucked us into its orbit and is dragging us steadily down to disaster.

II Peter 3:17 warns,

You therefore, beloved, knowing this beforehand, be on your guard lest, being carried away by the error of unprincipled men, you fall from your own steadfastness (NASV).

It is not the godly men who are leading the new music trend. It is the "unprincipled," the carnally-minded who have their arms around the world and are telling us this is the way it is supposed to be. We are told to guard ourselves lest we be carried

---

[1] Dave Hendricks, *Successful Broadcasting in the Seventies*, Religious Broadcasting. Feb./March, 1978, p. 25.

away by the same error.

We Are Conforming

In Psalm 34:3 David exclaims,

> O magnify the Lord with me and let us exalt His name together.

This, too, should be our goal in music as well as in other areas of our Christian experience. But much of the music that some are claiming glorifies and exalts God cannot because it is only an imitation of the world's fleshly music. The biblical admonition of Romans 12:1, "be not conformed to this world," is as valid today as it was in Paul's day. Somehow we make excuses to continue on with our practices, always believing that worldliness is something other than what we are engaged in. Is copying worldly music styles conforming to the world? Does God not mean what He says?

Most of the new music is youth oriented. As one writer puts it, "At last we have some music that young people can identify with." And now an entire generation that has grown up on rock music can have their cake and eat it too.

Some items:

Record Companies Lead The Way

In a 1972 article, "Survey of Christian Musicals," Eternity magazine music editor Richard Stanislaw reviews some of the then fledgling youth musicals: "There is no longer any 'if' about the impact of popular music in churches today."[1] Then he lists a sampling of the new musicals along with a brief description of their contents:

---

[1]Eternity, August, 1972, p. 47.

Ted Smith's Requiem for a Nobody: *"There are touches of Simon and Garfunkle, Carole King, Dionne Warwick, Glen Campbell."*

The Carpenter *". . . uses 1940's night club sounds, 1950's country blues, 1960's ballads and 1970's acid rock."*

John Peterson's The Good Life *". . . is a Broadway imitation modeled after South Pacific or Oklahoma."*

Mr. Stanislaw suggests purchasing an "instrumental-only" music track to use as background for your local production. Professionally done, *"Singspiration offers Lawrence Welk sounds."*

Item: From The Latest Word, published by Word Record Company, advertising two recent releases (Spring 1977):

Sunday Trombones Pay Tribute to Andre Crouch: *"Offers mellow tones not unlike those achieved by the best instrumentalists in big bands a generation ago."*

The Music Machine, *"A Musical Adventure Teaching The Fruit of the Spirit To All Ages,"* is on the Children's Religious Best Sellers list. Musically, it combines Rock, Folk Rock, Jazz, Blues and Broadway.

Sunday Saxes Pay Tribute to Bill Gaither:
"*The style resembles that of Billy Vaughn
and Guy Lombardo.*"

**Imitating
Broadway**

Obvious imitations of Broadway musicals,
the music of the big band era and the
styles of Lawrence Welk, Glen Campbell,
Billy Vaughn, and Dionne Warwick are in
direct contrast to scriptural commands:

*I beseech you, therefore, brethren,
by the mercies of God,
    that ye present your bodies
    a living sacrifice,
    holy, acceptable unto God,
which is
your reasonable service.*
(Romans 12:1)

*Love not the world,
    neither the things
    that are in the world.
If any man love the world,
    the love of the Father
    is not in him.*
(1 John 2:15)

*Wherefore,
come out from among them,
and be ye separate,
    saith the Lord,
and touch not the unclean thing;
    and I will receive you.*
(2 Corinthians 6:17)

But the arrangers, performers, and
publishers will continue to produce this
music as long as the Christian public will
docilely go on accepting it as the "new

music for the new age" and pay money for the product.

Item: William Peterson writes enthusiastically about these youth musicals,

> In large civic auditoriums, slick folk musicals with an unmistakable rock beat are premiering before crowds of 5,000 and 10,000 people, and when the invitation is given hundreds of people respond. . . . There's no doubt about it, God is working through contemporary music today.

He cites the example of a youth director who had been having difficulty getting his young people interested in the traditional youth choir. "When they decided to put on Tell It Like It Is, they discovered that they had more young people than they could use. . . . Young people from all over the city packed out the church, and that night 200 people responded to the invitation at the close of the service."[1]

This musical, by Ralph Carmichael and Kurt Kaiser, which sold 300,000 copies in its first three years, is another Broadway imitation with all the glitter and sounds of a New York original. It is not difficult to see why these musicals are popular. Walking the narrow path of a life consecrated to Christ does not have the appeal of the groovy Christian life as depicted in these productions. (See Chapter 14 for a further discussion of Tell

---

[1]William Peterson, A New Day for Christian Music, The Wesleyan Advocate, Sept. 16, 1974, p. 6.

it *Like it is.*)

Item: Another method being used to try to reach unchurched youth are radio programs which take their cue from the rock programs that are heard on the same stations.

A Warped Gospel

The Scott Ross Show, produced by a young former disc jockey who believes that *"you'll never reach young people with the Third Church of the Frigidaire approach,"* uses rock, jazz, blues, country, folk, and classical as a bridge, then comments on these songs in terms of the gospel. The program has won Billboard Magazine's top award for a religious type program.

What's it All About, emceed by a Presbyterian minister and former disc jockey, uses rock as a springboard. Records are picked from top selling secular charts. He has won a *"Gabriel"* for *"the best youth oriented program for a national broadcast."*

Both the Billboard and the *"Gabriel"* awards are given by secular organizations. Jesus said, *"Woe unto you when all men speak well of you . . ."* (Luke 6:26).

Powerline uses Top 40 tunes and comments on them in terms of evangelism. A fast talking disc jockey who imitates the D.J.'s on secular rock stations delivers the dialogue. Says a Powerline spokesman, *"We're meeting the needs of young people without being preachy."* (Christ is the need of young people. How can this message be gotten across without preaching?)

Sounds of Joy plays the latest contemporary gospel records. It includes interviews and short "drop-in" thoughts that may interest teen-agers. The philosophy of this program is, "We cannot reach youth, Christian or non-Christian, with traditional church music."

The setting up of their own standards ("you'll never reach young people unless...," etc.) is not unusual for those who are trying to interest young people in the gospel with the Madison Avenue approach. Sincere as they may be, those who use these methods are substituting human philosophy and effort for simple obedience to God's Word.

A Welcome Contrast

In contrast to these programs is Teen Tempo, produced by a teen-age brother and sister team, Arla and Dave Bott. Their format is different. Explains Dave,

> "The popular theory today takes for granted that all Christian teen-ager programming must, without question, involve a rock sound in order to produce a valid format that makes such programming relevant. I say nonsense."

An interesting statement coming from a member of the generation they say cannot be reached unless it is done with their own music.

3

CASHING IN ON CHRISTIAN MUSIC

Many secular pop stars claim the salvation experience. They are cashing in on our gullibility by traveling about the country appearing at youth meetings and Christian television programs while at the same time happily riding the night club circuit.

* * *

Not many years ago Christians would have been embarrassed to have been mentioned as participating in questionable TV shows. Today's trend is to glory in it.

* * *

Today we have Christian "stars" doing their thing, with all the glamour and build-up of a Hollywood celebrity, and without apology.

* * *

Has Satan so blinded us that we can no longer discern right from wrong?

CASHING IN ON CHRISTIAN MUSIC

The Trend Setters

Since 1975, a *Christian Artists Music Seminar* has been held during the summer in Estes Park, Colorado.

Their recent Seminar was billed as a:

> . . . *fantastic festival of learning, inspiration and fellowship with the world's greatest Christian artists and clinicians. . . .*

Pictured on the advertising brochure, along with a short personal sketch, are several featured seminar participants. These are the leaders, the trend-setters, the big names of Christian music today.

Here are some excerpts from the brochure:

> _____ Lead soloist and star of television return of *Your Hit Parade.*
>
> _____ has performed on numerous major network shows including *The Donny and Marie Show, Sonny and Cher, Glen Campbell, Bob Hope, Tonight Show,* and many more.
>
> _____ Host of several radio shows, television and movie actor including *Hawaii Five-O* and *Camelot.*

Looking for a night club act? This looks as if this is the place to find it.

**Enter
Christian
"Stars"**

Noticeably missing from the promotional rhetoric is any mention of a Christian commitment or details you would like to know if you were going to invite them to your church or youth conference. Not many years ago Christians would have been embarrassed to have been mentioned as participating on these shows or to have any close association with the entertainment world. Today's trend is to glory in it. These are the Christian "stars" doing their thing, with all the glamour and build-up of a Hollywood celebrity, and without apology.

Somehow it doesn't measure up to the New Testament standard of Christianity. There are no *"stars"* mentioned in the Bible. Jesus said, *"If any man will follow me, let him deny himself and take up his cross daily"* (Luke 9:23).

Has Satan so blinded us that we can no longer discern right from wrong? Or maybe it is easier to blame Satan than to admit that we have left the truth and are pursuing our own fleshly desires and interests.

**Hitting
Big-Time
Christian
TV**

Further examples of the lack of discernment are the many secular pop stars who have claimed a salvation experience. They are cashing in on our gullibility by traveling about the country appearing at youth meetings and Christian television programs while at the same time happily riding the night club circuit. One such star has a number of Christian songs to his name and has appeared in large Christian gatherings to share his *"testimony."*

"I find myself evil. I believe in the devil as much as God. You can use either one to get things done."—Peter Criss, Kiss.

KISS, a popular rock group of the late 1970's, even reached the young bubble gum generation with **KISS** bubble gum cards. The packet contained a 1" X 3" sliver of bubble gum and 7 **KISS** cards.

In his *"other life"* he is a superstar pop singer and actor in R-rated movies.

A few days ago while driving along in my car, I was flipping the radio dial, trying to find some good music. I caught the name of _____, another superstar entertainer who has shared the platform with many well-known Christians. Since it was a country-western station, I wasn't too interested in leaving it on. Suddenly the announcer gave the name of the song and _____ was singing before I could flip the dial again. The song could only be described as immoral.

That the lives of these individuals are sometimes a contradiction of purposes does not seem to offend many Christians who continue to support them by buying their songs and records or by paying $5-$10 a ticket to hear them perform.

Rock Operas Emerge

It is this lack of discernment that allows Christians to be taken in by such blatant error as the two religious rock operas that came out in the early 70's—Jesus Christ Superstar and Godspell. Though they have come and made their millions, and now are fading, we ought to examine them to see what they have to offer believers.

Superstar was produced first. Within two years it had grossed over $62 million. The original recording and the movie sound track together have sold more than eight million copies. Superstar has been staged in 16 countries.

In the movie version, Jesus is presented as a hippie-type who is followed around by a covey of harlots. Mary Magdalene, dressed as ε harlot, sings suggestively, *"I don't know how to love Him."* The last supper is portrayed as a picnic, and the real hero turns out to be Judas.

John The Baptist Smoking Cigar

Godspell is supposedly based on the gospel of Matthew. It depicts Christ as a clown, complete with a Superman sweatshirt. The action takes place in a New York junk yard. He is *"baptized"* with a sponge by John the Baptist (who in one scene is shown floating in a swimming pool, smoking a cigar) and is crucified on a wire fence.

One need not be a theologian nor even a Christian to see that there is no connection between the truth of Christ's deity as revealed in the gospels and the blasphemous rock versions of His life. Yet some Christians, many of whom are bent on communicating with the world, are somehow fooled into believing that these productions are relevant.

There is a paradox in this: While many Christian people defended *Superstar* and *Godspell*, many unbelievers saw through the facade.

A debate might line up something like this:

SUPERSTAR

FOR

Bill Pearce/Musician

People say it is anti-Christian in spirit and approach and contains a mixture of truth and error. This may be so, but I think "Superstar" opens the door if it does nothing more than speak of Christ's humanity.

Ron Hutchcraft
Youth for Christ Int.

It is turning the attention of thousands of kids to Jesus Christ.

AGAINST

Tim Rice/Superstar librettist

"Superstar" says Christ was a remarkable man and that's really as far as it goes.

Harold Schonberg/music critic for the New York Times

"Superstar" is a piece of junk masquerading as relevance.

Time Magazine

"Jesus Christ Superstar" is a tasteless, morally offensive, carnival-type show that exploits one of the most elevating episodes in man's history for the purpose of making a lot of money.

GODSPELL

FOR	AGAINST
Mel White/film producer	John-Michael Tabelok writer of *Godspell*.
The "Godspell" cast really gave us new glasses to view, understand, and enjoy the gospel.	*Be it Jesus or Krishna—the message is the same.*
Christianity Today	Clive Barnes New York Columnist
"Godspell" could well be one of the best ways to reach kids with the gospel. . . .	*Jesus is made into a pure simpleton clown.*
	A *Seattle Times* music critic -
Right On (A Jesus Rock publication)	After attending a production by a local Christian college, called it "blasphemy."
See the show. Take a bunch of Sunday school kids along or a minister and expose yourself to the living reality.	The South African government, in spite of the churches' objections, banned both "Superstar" and "Godspell" because they were "offensive."

Who is on whose side?
The early Christians turned the world upside down.
Today the world has turned Christians upside down.

4

HOW DID IT ALL HAPPEN?

The prevailing attitude seemed to be, *"if you want to win them you've got to identify with them — use their language, dress as they do, use their music."*

* * *

And into the church came rock and all the rest of the world's music.

* * *

The corruption in church music is a reflection of the instability even of today's Bible-believing churches. This is evil.

* * *

What has taken place in the past 15 years that has caused church music to join hands with the world?

4

HOW DID IT ALL HAPPEN?

The Subtle Trend

What has taken place in the past 15 years that has caused church music to join hands with the world?

While Christian music had, for several years, been slowly on the decline, it wasn't until the 1960's that the flood gates were pushed wide open. For years liberal educators, sociologists and clergymen had promoted the idea of individual freedom of expression. During the 60's this idea began to bear its fruit. The Great Society became the permissive society. It was freedom, but freedom without restraints.

Decade Of Rebellion

It all started with some harmless (as some thought) *"flower children"* in San Francisco and culminated in a period of youth rebellion and revolution unparalleled in our nation's history. Mass demonstrations, riots and burning in the 60's caused millions of dollars worth of property damage all over the country. The street mob was yelling *"burn, baby, burn."* College students were demanding changes in the academic process and if their demands weren't met, they stormed their presidents' offices or bombed administration buildings.

Vietnam, Kent State, Berkeley and Watts made the headlines daily as they were, for the youthful rebels, the fuel that fed the revolutionary fires. Drugs began to flow like water. And rock music, with its "do your own thing" philosophy, became the battle cry of thousands of rebellious young people.

The Counterculture

From out of this came the counterculture, a completely youth-oriented society with its own leaders and its own morality. It was the counterculture that dictated to the rest of society that hair would be long and skirts short, that chastity was no longer a desired commodity, that teenagers would wear jeans and T-shirts to school and that homework and discipline were out.

Parents didn't know what to do. Those who were supposed to know—the educators, sociologists and clergy—pressed the panic button. Their solution was to communicate with them at all costs "or lose them." Many sincere and well-meaning Christians got caught in the tide. Concessions were made. Attracting and keeping young people interested became the church's consuming concern. The prevailing attitude seemed to be, "if you want to win them you've got to identify with them —use their language, dress as they do, use their music." And into the church came rock and all the rest of the world's music.

Rock Music Is BIG BUSINESS
by Salem Kirban

In 1964 the Beatles introduced Rock music. It's been with us ever since. And it's big business. While no complete record of earnings is available, former Beatle John Lennon's fortune is said to include more than $150 Million in real estate holdings alone!

The Beatles top record album sold about 10 million units in the United States. But this has been surpassed by the Bee Gees. Saturday Night Fever—the soundtrack of the movie featuring the Bee Gees' music—has sold more than 15 Million copies, and over 27 Million worldwide, Fortune magazine reports. (Fortune, April 23, 1979)

Sales of records and tapes in the United States is rapidly approaching an annual $5 BILLION in sales at the retail level! From hard rock, punk rock to soft rock, pop rock and folk rock . . . has come Disco. Disco has a pulsating beat (about 120 thumps per minute).

A company's average up-front investment in a rock album has risen from about $100,000 to, now, close to One Quarter Million Dollars! Superstars like Paul Simon (originally of Simon & Garfunkel) and Paul McCartney can demand as high as $2 Million to make an album. To break even a record company would have to sell 2 million records of McCartney's Wings group. Once they did sell the 2 million . . . McCartney would receive an additional 22% royalty rate on additional sales. This is nearly $2 on every $8.98 album.

Top Rock stars make an incredible annual income. A British group called Pink Floyd made $20 Million last year. One album, "The Wall," sold an astounding **one million copies a day** worldwide. Pink Floyd group makes so much money on record sales that they rarely give concerts.

Income by other Rock stars include:

The Eagles	$7.5 Million
Led Zeppelin	4.5 Million
Supertramp	4.4 Million
Fleetwood Mac	3.0 Million
Paul McCartney	2.7 Million
The Rolling Stones	2.4 Million
The Who	2 Million

The head of one Rock group said:

> *Our music is intended to broaden the generation gap, to alienate children from their parents, and to prepare people for the revolution.*

Rock music appeals to the body's glands and sensuous nature. *"Christian Rock"* is essentially spiritual fornication. The low frequency vibrations of the bass guitar ... the driving beat of the drum have a direct effect on the pituitary gland. The pituitary gland produces hormones that control the sexual responses of male and female. With the incessant beat of Rock music, a radical imbalance occurs in the brain. The end effect is an overload of hormones that can cause moral inhibitions to either drop or be wiped out completely.

There have been several Christian Concert Promotion Seminars and Showcase conventions held recently. One of their leaders publishes a newsletter in which he writes, in part:

> Jesus *"Rock"* is definitely maturing into the accepted lingua franca *(a hybrid language)* for this generation of Christians.
>
> It is no longer a fad, and while it will always offend the *"Graham Generation,"* it must be used as an integral part of all efforts to evangelize the young adult culture which now dominates the American society.
>
> This will happen in two ways:
>
> **(1)** As contemporary Christian music is allowed to become the grass-roots medium for worship and local evangelism; and
>
> **(2)** As more professional artists are used for major special events like telecast rock concerts, rallies, and weekend *"Jesus festivals."*
>
> ... we must organize efforts to train a cadre of new young artists—and support people like promoters who will help them with a ministry of music. This can be done by supporting new associations, seminars, and events aimed at them. Concert promoters and contemporary musicians need to learn how to build a network of support ... and donor constituency.
>
> ... we must form *"new"* contemporary churches that will feed these, His sheep.

Not only is it important that we become aware of the inroads contemporary music is making in the church ... but we must actively encourage our young people to becoming discerning Christians.

**Rock
Music
Here
To Stay**

Today, the burnings are a thing of the past. Vietnam is just an unpleasant memory. College campuses are quiet. Students are more interested in pursuing their own private world of pleasure than in political issues or in tossing the president out on the sidewalk. Most of the rebel leaders have quietly joined the establishment. But the music that began in the *counterculture* and was the marching-song of the movement is now firmly implanted in the church.

This lamentable situation may be summed up with this statement by Torrey Johnson, founder of Youth for Christ. After attending a concert by an evangelical national youth organization that included rock sounds, he observed sadly, *"The corruption in church music is a reflection of the instability even of today's Bible-believing churches. This is evil."*[1]

---

[1]The Evangel, June 1971, p. 8.

5
THE POWER OF MUSIC

In the 18th century French dentists traveled from town to town in wagons. Most of them carried small orchestras with them. This served two purposes.

* * *

When the little boy played, the seizures abated and the governor would resume his normal activities, only to send for Chopin again when the musical medicine wore off.

* * *

At Northwestern University students listened to both jazz and Bach for 25 consecutive days. The purpose was to observe the reaction to musical form and completeness.

At the end of the 25 days the students were polled, *"Which music did you prefer?"* The answer was very surprising!

5

THE POWER OF MUSIC

**Music
Influential**

Through the ages man has realized that music not only gives pleasure and enjoyment through listening, it has power to control our minds and bodies as well.

> *For changing peoples' manners and altering their customs there is nothing better than music.*
> Shu Ching 6th Century B.C.

> *Music doth extenuate fears, furies, appeaseth cruelty, abateth heaviness and to such as are wakeful it causeth quiet rest; it cures all irksomeness and heaviness of the soul.*
> Cassiodarus, The Divine Letters, about A.D. 550

> *Music is an essential and necessary function of man. It influences his behavior and condition and has done so for thousands of years.*
> Thayer Gaston, Musical Therapist, 1968

David, the young shepherd who was skilled on the harp, played for King Saul. The evil spirit that was troubling Saul departed and he was refreshed in his spirit.

**Music
Affects
Body
Functions**

Pythagoras, the famous mathematician and philosopher of 25 centuries ago, was also a musician of accomplishment. He is usually accredited with the discovery of the diatonic scale and the correct measurement of musical intervals. He believed

> that music could be divided into **three** parts: rhythm, melody and harmony. Pythagoras taught that rhythm was associated with the physical life and the functions of the body; melody with man's psychic being, emotional and mental; and harmony with his spiritual existence.[1]

Much of today's research on the effect of music on our lives has had its origins with this Pythagorean theory. During medieval times

> physicians frequently called in minstrels to play and sing to convalescing patients. The beneficial effects of soothing melody were carefully observed and it was noted that fears and worries which usually accompany serious ailments responded to gentle melodies which relieved the tendency of the sufferer to dwell upon his own condition.[2]

It was also customary to entertain expectant mothers with the lute. It was believed that soothing music had a beneficial ef-

---

[1]Manly P. Hall, *The Therapeutic Value of Music* (The Philosophical Research Society, 1955), p. 17.
[2]Ibid., p. 6.

fect on both the mother and the unborn child.

Music In The Dentist's Chair

In the 18th century French dentists traveled from town to town in wagons. Most of them carried small orchestras with them. This served two purposes: The music attracted customers, and in the place of anesthesia the orchestra played loudly, distracting the patient from the pain. When a troublesome tooth needed to be pulled the rumble of the drums and clanging of cymbals came at the appropriate moment.

Two hundred years later, in the 1960's, modern dentists were experimenting with essentially the same method, only in place of the live orchestra was electronically controlled music. The technique was known as audio-analgesia. Instead of a local anesthesia the patient was hooked up with earphones. Taped music, or a *"white"* sound, was then played as the dentist began his work. A control device which regulated the volume was placed in the patient's lap. When the pain began he merely increased the sound. It worked with the majority of patients. The theory was that the music acted as an *"interrupter"* of the pain's message to the brain. It transferred the patient's attention to the sound through some subconscious means. Just about the time this method was gaining favor among dentists, someone began to wonder just how much volume a person could take before he went deaf. Ear drums are delicate and can be easily damaged by loud noises. Exit the audio-analgesia technique.

**Music
An Ancient
Cure For
Depression**

Frederic Chopin, in the early 1800's, was to become the greatest pianist of his day and composer of some of the world's greatest piano music. At the age of ten, he was frequently requested to play for the Grand Duke Constantine, governor of Poland. The Duke had recurring seizures of madness which could seemingly be controlled only by Chopin's music. When the little boy played, the seizures abated and the governor could resume his normal activities, only to send for Chopin again when the musical medicine wore off.

**Music
Stimulates
Sales**

In modern times the possibility of controlling the behavior of groups of people with music began to intrigue corporation owners and business heads. Would it be possible to influence the buying habits of customers? Enterprising executives hired psychologists and musicians to do some experimenting. The result? Walk into almost any supermarket or other business and what greets you? Music! Why do they play it? For the enjoyment of the customer? Partly. But they have found that the right type of music, played at the right time of day at the right volume, can stimulate people to purchase more. The poor customer doesn't have a chance! Like Ulysses, who had himself tied to the mast of his ship lest he yield to the beckoning voices of the Sirens and be dashed to pieces on the rocks, the customer needs to have a firm grip on his pocketbook as he enters the store.

A few months ago I noticed that one of our local drugstores had begun using music. I

A study in contrasts as three girls watch a Rock concert. Do we seek the same sensual, physical thrills in the *"Now Christian sound"*?

asked the druggist why. He replied that previously when someone would come in, especially if it was early and he was the only shopper, the silence could be frightening. I suppose the customer imagined he could hear the salesgirl tapping her foot, impatiently waiting for him to hurry up and buy something. Now, with music, that has all changed. Even a lone customer is more relaxed and takes his time.

In doctors' and dentists' offices soft music is played in order to calm the fears associated with people in white coats, with trays of long needles and imposing looking instruments.

Music Increases Work Production

Industry, too, has seen the benefits of using music. One of the earliest studies ever made to prove the positive influences of music on factory workers was during a six day bicycle race held at Madison Square Garden in 1910. Among the spectators was a plant manager. He noticed that every other race was accompanied by band music. He noted also that during the race that was accompanied by the band the cyclists were working at maximum effort. He concluded that it must have something to do with the music. Rushing out to buy a stopwatch, he returned to do some calculating. When the band was playing the racers averaged 19.6 mph. For the races that had no music the average was 17.9 mph. He judged that the band had a decided effect on the cyclists even after six days of riding.

During World War II music was being put to another important use. Many men returning home from months of front line combat were suffering from battle fatigue. In extreme cases the nervous system was completely broken down, leaving the G.I. out of touch with reality.

At the Army Medical Center in Washington D.C. a pilot program was introduced that was hoped would offer help through the therapeutic properties of music. Patients were put on a program that included listening to soothing, sedative music as well as participating in music.

Music As Therapy

Here is the account of one officer who was treated with sound rather than drugs:

A 30 year old lieutenant was admitted following a long tour of combat duty. He was very depressed and completely obsessed with the memories of the war. A diagnosis of schizophrenia was made. Because of his deep inward depression, music of a stimulating nature was prescribed. It was found that he was allergic to jazz. His progress at first was slow.

Gradually be began to relate to the musician who daily played the piano for him. In three weeks of sessions he was well enough to be discharged to his own care.[1]

In the 3½ year study at the Medical Center the lieutenant was only one of many patients who were helped through

---

[1] Emil A. Gutheil, *Music and Your Emotions* (Liveright, 1952), p. 48.

Music In Special Education

music. Not all recoveries were as quick or as successful as his, but it did lead the researchers to conclude "that a systematic and skillful application of music in neuro-psychiatric hospitals has proved to be a definite adjunct to the psychiatric regime.[1] Or in laymen's terms: Music does the job!

Today music therapy is being used widely in a variety of situations as standard procedure, both practical and experimental.

Ditson used moderate background music during regularly scheduled therapy sessions with cerebral palsied children. *"Over a period of 70 sessions he found a marked increase in the activities and the display of socially acceptable behavior."*[2]

Dreikus and Crocker worked with psychotic children who exhibited little or no appropriate emotional responses. Seeing improvement in their behavior after a music program was instituted they concluded *"that music, as a means of communication, may be used profitably as an aid to eliciting better emotional responses."*[3]

In a special education school, background music was used with severely retarded girls who were autistic, schizophrenic or epileptic. The clinical worker reported that their behavior, which had been erratic, had, since the introduction of music, improved. The music also had a

---

[1]*Ibid.*, p. 53.
[2]E. Thayer Gaston, Music in Therapy (The Macmillan Co., 1968), p. 140.
[3]*Ibid.*, p. 177.

Soft Music Has Soothing Effect

therapeutic effect on the employees. Working with juvenile delinquents held in detention, Lindecker's study showed that when music was playing in the background *"they seemed to lose much of their physical and emotional tension."*[1]

Sears found that listening to sedative music reduced muscle tension 99% of the time. Kraukow, experimenting with the effect of music on the eyes, believed that a listener's eyesight could be improved as

[1]E. Thayer Gaston, *Music in Therapy* (The MacMillan Company, 1968), p. 177

Music is also used in fast food restaurants to encourage you to hurry through your meal so there is a rapid turnover of customers. Next time you eat, listen how the music changes from slow to rapid. You'll flip through your french fries and make short work of your sundae in three minutes flat.

much as 25%. Scientists have also discovered that music has an effect on posture and that listening to soft music helps digestion.

Today music is being used in an increasing number of industries and businesses. Through experimenting it has been found that a simple and familiar melody carried mostly in the strings and not overbearing in the brass or percussion is most acceptable.

It should be played at a level that is discernible but not so as to interfere with work or conversation. Benefits noted on individual employees have been less tension while on the job and less fatigue at the end of the day. These benefits are passed on to the employee's family. Relaxed and rested, he is less likely to yell at his wife and children when he gets home.

Schools Experiment With Background Music

Schools and colleges are also making use of background music. Though the program is relatively new, it is producing good results.

At Stanford University's School of Education a study of background music was made to see if it benefited students. They reported,

> It can be stated that when high school students are exposed to background music of a sophisticated nature, their attitude toward school will be more positive than when they are not exposed to such music.[1]

---

[1] *Background Music In Schools* (3M Background Music Systems, St. Paul, 1967), p. 3.

**Students
More
Orderly**

Cited were a number of instances. When music was played in hallways during breaks between classes, students were more orderly. In libraries and study halls music masks distracting noises, making it easier to concentrate. In counselling and guidance centers music puts students more at ease and has a calming influence.

At Northwestern University students with no music background were asked to listen to both jazz and Bach for 25 consecutive days. The purpose was to observe the reaction to musical form and completeness. At the end of the 25 days the students were polled, *"Which music did you prefer?"* There was unanimous agreement. They preferred Bach. His music was the more satisfying. The jazz, they said, *"was too much like the confusion of everyday living to be ultimately satisfying."*[1]

---

[1]William Lloyd Hooper, *Church Music In Transition* (Broadman Press, 1963), p. 168.

6

THE LONE RANGER, SUPERMARKETS AND YOU

Did you know that cows give more milk and chickens lay better eggs when they listen to music?

* * *

One researcher exposed plants to two types of music—soft classical and acid rock. At the end of the experiment the results were astounding!

* * *

A missionary took back to Africa with him records of semi-classical music and acid rock. He played both to members of the local tribe. Again, the results confirmed previous tests!

* * *

In one experiment, a teen-age boy and girl sat in a room. Neither had met before. Several types of music were piped in the room and their reactions were studied. The investigators did turn up some interesting things about the effect of music on the emotions, to say nothing of the romantic inclinations of a teen-age boy and girl!

6

THE LONE RANGER, SUPERMARKETS AND YOU

Music Affects Animals And Plants

Did you know that cows give more milk and chickens lay better eggs when they listen to music? I asked several farmers who regularly play music in barns and chicken houses if this was true. The response was unanimous. It works. Somehow even cows and hens are more relaxed when they are exposed to music.

You have probably read about various experiments conducted to see how plants might respond to music. One researcher exposed plants to two types—soft classical and acid rock. At the end of the experiment the plants exposed to soft music were flourishing. But those exposed to the acid rock had all wilted and died.

The conclusion was that some musical vibrations could have positive effects while others could be detrimental.

Some people are beginning to think that plants even have feelings. One woman said she developed friendships with hers. She talked to them and they responded by producing better leaves and fruit. When she didn't "visit" with them they seemed disappointed and began to droop.

I had better stop reading things like that. I'm beginning to feel guilty about weeding my garden.

Music . . .
A Mood
Changer

Bob Larson, in his book, Rock and Roll: The Devil's Diversion, tells of this experiment: A missionary took back to Africa with him records of semi-classical music and acid rock. He played both to members of the local tribe. When the semi-classical was played the people responded with smiles and nods of approval and were generally calm and peaceful. Then without comment he switched to the rock. Immediately their expressions changed. They became confused and agitated. Some grabbed their spears and were ready for war. Others sized up the situation and threw rocks at the record player. All this just by changing the music. The change in their behavior was a natural reaction to the music.

Phil Kerr, (from Music in Evangelism) cites an experiment as reported by Mr. Arthur Cremin, president of The American Creative League of Music. The unsuspecting "guinea pigs" were a teenage boy and girl. They had never met previously and were completely unaware of any strange happenings. Unfortunately for them, as they sat getting acquainted in

Music changes moods subtly but effectively.

a cozy *"private"* room with soft music playing in the background, their reactions were being observed and recorded (all in the interest of science, of course). When classical music and soft ballads were piped into the room they talked and were friendly, but somewhat aloof. When pop music and jazz were played they quickly developed a much *"friendlier"* attitude and began to hold hands and put their arms around each other. When the music changed back to classical and ballads they would again become more formal and reserved. If the music would swing back to the jazz and pop music *"their formality would give way to familiarity."*[1]

The investigators did turn up some interesting things about the effect of music on the emotions, to say nothing of the romantic inclinations of a teen-age boy and girl!

Similar Effects On Large Groups

To find out how large groups of people would respond to the same music Dr. Alexander Capruso (1948, director of the School of Music, Syracuse University) tested over a thousand non-music students. He used several different types of recordings and played them for groups of 100 or more. He found that the mood of an entire group could be changed by changing the music. Another researcher went even further. Bigham tested over 20,000 persons. He used 90 different records. The results, he found, were essentially the same as Dr. Capruso's.

---

[1] Phil Kerr, *Music in Evangelism* (Gospel Music Publishers, 1939), p. 19.

Since so many people were having fun with their experiments I decided to try one of my own. I chose 13 contrasting pieces of music and put them on tape. The tape was then played for two of my largest classes (60-70 students). The students were asked to write down their impressions.

"What comes to your mind?" "How does the music make you feel?" "What does this piece say to you?"

When the results were tabulated there was a uniformity to their answers. Again, proof that music can control the mood of large groups of people. There was one answer that still puzzles me, however. One girl commented as she listened to a certain selection, *"I see Bugs Bunny conducting an orchestra."* (I think she had been watching too much television!)

Music A Tempo Control

A Texas cafeteria owner who employs an organist to play during the lunch hour likes to show friends how the music can control the tempo of patrons going through the serving line. When the organist plays a slow waltz the line moves slowly. People take their time making their meal selections. When he switches to a fast march the line speeds up and the customers take much less time filling their trays. If he drops back to the slow tempo the line does the same.

All the while no one in the serving line has the slightest hint that the man seated innocently at the console is, at his will, controlling their actions.

Radio, movies and T.V. have, since their beginnings, specialized in creating moods by the use of background music. Even before "talkies" came along, theater audiences were kept on the edge of their seats as the villain rode off with a frightened Little Lulu and William S. Hart in hot pursuit. From the dimly lit orchestra pit came the dramatic sounds of a badly out of tune piano responding to the nimble fingers of the pianist as he pounded out the accompaniment to the action on the screen.

The Lone Ranger

Remember this famous line, *"From out of the past come the thundering hoofs of the great white horse Silver"*? You probably do if you were born in this century. Even if you don't you would recognize without hesitation the theme song that follows the legendary call, *"Hi yo Silver, Away."* That it was part of Rossini's William Tell Overture didn't matter. To you it was simply the introduction to *The Lone Ranger.*

Music Changes Moods

During the late 30's and early 40's millions of kids immediately upon hearing that opening trumpet call would drop what they were doing (hopefully it wasn't the dishes) and make a dash for the radio. That theme, in a flash, brought visions of cowboys, Indians and the old West. Every radio program had its own special theme song. There was The Green Hornet, Sergeant Preston of the Yukon, Little Orphan Annie, Jack Armstrong, Sky King, Shafter Parker and His Circus, Gangbusters and many more. The mood for the adventure to follow was set by that open-

Worshiper dances in the aisle with Chaplain at a communion service in the Perkins Chapel at Southern Methodist University in Dallas, Texas.

ing theme. Most programs also included exciting music during the hour to reinforce the drama. The mind would take over from there.

Background Music In Films And Television

Today background music for films and T.V. is used much the same way. A nature film, for instance, will require one type of music, a Western another and a documentary still another. Without music to set the mood for the action, the film would be missing a vital element. The viewer, in order to become a part of what he is watching, needs the tension building or calming sound. Sometime just turn down the audio dial of your T.V. as you are watching and notice what happens. Beside missing the dialogue you will miss the background music which helps to put you in the proper mood. (Or better yet, turn the T.V. off altogether and read a good book.)

Talented musicians are paid large salaries to compose musical scores that will complement the action on the screen in order to keep you glued to the tube. T.V. networks must please their bosses—the companies that spend millions each year to plug their product on the prime time program they hope you will be watching. Music plays a definite part. Obviously it can be a powerful ally to suggestion.

Making A Sound Track

Let's go behind the scenes for a moment and see how a score for a film might be developed. The composer first views the film several times to get the *"feel"* of it. Then he decides what music would be appropriate to accompany the action. The sound will be dubbed in later. This serves a practical purpose. An actor who can't sing can silently mouth the words during the filming, then a singer who can't act can "sync" the lip movements later in the studio.

After deciding what will fit the action the composer chooses his materials as carefully as an artist would choose his colors. Like the artist the composer paints pictures—only these pictures are aural rather than visual. He has at his disposal all of the musical elements that will create in the viewer the required response. Involved along the way will be orchestrators, conductors, the orchestra and a parade of soundmen and electronic equipment. The completed scene along with the music then might go something like this:

The Tender Scene

On the screen we see the hero and heroine saying a tender and moving good-bye. What would you expect to hear in the background? A cymbal crash and a hard wallop on the bass drum? Hardly. A

trumpet fanfare? Not unless the cavalry is about to charge the house. The accompanying music must not detract from the drama. The music for this scene probably will be soft and slow and feature muted violins or a flute played *sotto voce*.

The drama is touching. The music is beautifully sentimental. The desired effect is produced and the audience cries.

The Tense Scene

Now let's change the scene. We are back in the hero's apartment. He's hungry and decides to go to the kitchen for a ham sandwich. Unknown to him the meanest gorilla of the zoo has escaped, entered the house and this moment is hiding in the kitchen. The audience knows it. The gorilla knows it. But the hero doesn't. As he walks unsuspectingly across the living room (the hero, not the gorilla), the music in the background begins to crescendo and build up tension. Flash to the kitchen. The gorilla is waiting. Back to the hero. He's getting nearer to the kitchen door. Near . . . nearer . . . . The music is getting intense. The hero pushes open the door and—brass, **fortissimo agitato!**

Let's try that scene again. This time without music. Our hero crosses the room. No music. No build-up. No suspense. He opens the kitchen door. Silence. He sees the intruder—and wonders why there is a gorilla in his kitchen. He walks calmly to the refrigerator for his ham sandwich.

Now let's repeat it once more, this time with the Brahms Lullaby playing in the background. No good. That won't do either. The music must be there and it must support the action.

**Music
Controls
Emotions**

You may not have noticed because you were too busy watching. But this is the way the composer often gets you in the mood with background music. These are some tested and tried methods:

Scene	Musical background
Ships on the high sea	French horns with dramatic air
Doting grandfather	Crackling bassoon in the low register
Suspense	Strings playing fast tremolo
Clown takes a fall	Muted trombone imitating laugh, "Wah, wah, wah."

So much for mood music.

The point of chapter six might simply be summed up this way: <u>Music can and does control our emotions, our actions and our attitudes</u>. Why is it necessary that we be aware of music's effect on us? If we can understand how music can stimulate us, relax us and influence our thinking, we will be able to better evaluate what we listen to and develop some valuable musical discrimination.

The next chapter will deal with the elements that do the controlling and how they work.

7

THE WAY IT WORKS

As you listen to a piece of music, though you are not aware of it, your entire body, including your nervous system, is constantly reacting to the sound.

* * *

Rhythm controls the activities of large groups. This is the reason why a disorganized mob can be turned into a unified body when someone begins a rhythmic chant and the rest pick it up.

* * *

Certain rhythms may affect more sensual bodily responses than others.

* * *

Pagan dances and rituals are always accompanied by the incessant beat of drums. Rhythm plays a major role in these demonic activities.

* * *

Dissonance is a clashing of harmonies. Dissonance in life and in music accounts for increases in nervous and psycho-neurotic ailments.

7

THE WAY IT WORKS

Your Unconscious Response To Music

As you listen to a piece of music, though you are not aware of it, your entire body, including your nervous system, is constantly reacting to the sound. Variations in pitch, rhythmic patterns, tempo and volume will affect pulse rate, blood pressure, respiration and the function of certain glands. These in turn will create a mood or elicit a physical response. Some music can make you relax and bring feelings of peace and contentment. Other music can cause frustration, nervousness or even depression. All of this comes as an automatic, subconscious response over which you have no control.

The Tension Release Factor

Why does it happen? Music, like the human body, consists of many tension-resolution or fulfillment situations. When we are hungry, we eat and are satisfied. If we are thirsty, we quench our thirst with a cool drink. If we are hot, we find shade.

If we are tired, we rest. These tensions require release. If they aren't released, more tension is built up and frustration sets in. It's something like a sneeze you feel coming on but doesn't arrive. You wait and wait. Frustration. Finally it happens. Ah, pure joy. What relief—real fulfillment.

Music Affects Body

Tension can even be experienced by proxy. Listen to a speaker who has a frog in his throat and you clear yours. How do you react when you hear a singer hang on and on to his final note? You begin to gasp for air. This is the tension-release factor.

Different musical sounds will affect different parts of the body. A high pitch will cause the larynx to tighten. Listen to a quick-step march, and you tap your foot. The fewer tensions in the music, the more calming effect it will have on the listener. This is one of the principles in using music for therapy. All music has some tension. Good music will have periods of tension but will follow with release and relaxation. Some types of music are mostly tension with very little relaxation. This builds frustration upon frustration which frequently finds its release in negative behavior—as we shall see in the next chapter.

We will be dealing with the more negative aspects of musical sounds in the next few chapters. For some background let's look at those factors that have the greatest influence in tension building. Though several things enter in, like extremes in volume, tempo, pitch and instrumental

Music can generate anger or nervous tension.

timbre, there are two elements that stand at the head of the class as major influences. They are rhythm and dissonance.

Rhythm Defined

Rhythm is the recurrence or repetition of a beat or sound usually occurring in a regular or harmonious pattern or manner. Rhythm is the energizer and organizer of music—its life-giving element. Without rhythm, music would be only a collection of stagnant sounds. Rhythm is the primary agent by which music stimulates and controls muscular action. It sets up tension which finds release in physical movement. That is why you tap your foot in time to a march. Strongly pulsed Sea Shanties were based upon the need for the sailors to pull together when hoisting the sails. A marching group needs a steady pulse of rhythm in order to keep in step. A rowing crew can't function without it.

Rhythm Controls Groups

Researchers have shown that

. . . it is the rhythm that controls the activities of large groups. . . . [It] furnishes a nonverbal persuasion not only to act but to act together."[1]

This is the reason why a disorganized mob can be turned into a unified body when someone begins a rhythmic chant and the rest pick it up. In response to a very rhythmic composition, especially if played very loud, a symphony audience will rise and give the orchestra a rousing ovation. The same audience will sit coughing and

[1]Gaston, op. cit., p. 19.

fidgeting through a piece with less moving rhythm and volume—much to the dismay of the conductor and orchestra.[1]

Rhythm And Muscular Strength

Strongly accented rhythms can actually create the capacity for muscular strength. Have you ever wondered why in pagan cultures men can dance for hours, sometimes all night, seemingly without becoming exhausted? Not discounting the reality of demonic activity, rhythm plays a major role. Pagan dances and rituals are always accompanied by the incessant beat of drums.

Strictly speaking, rhythm itself is not the "bad guy." All music has a natural flow of pulsations. When it becomes monotonous and repetitious, however, and if heavily accented and syncopated, it builds tension.

Sensual Bodily Responses

Though I have not found this substantiated in any experiments, it would seem that certain rhythms may affect more sensual bodily responses than others. To test this theory let's imagine we are listening to an afternoon band concert in the park. During the playing of the Washington Post March a young man sitting in the front row absently beats his foot in time to the stirring strains. On the repeat the band jazzes up the music (an abominable practice). The young man is now not only tapping his foot, he is swaying slightly to the

---

[1]Conductor Leopold Stokowski once became so infuriated with his hacking and wheezing audience that he stopped the orchestra, turned and began conducting the offensive patrons. "All right now, let's all cough together. 1-2-3-4, 1-2-3-4."

offbeat rhythms. The driving syncopation of jazz builds tension in a different part of the body,from when the music is played as originally written. Somehow these throbbing rhythms appeal to our base nature and the natural response is in sensual movements.

Rhythm Controls Body Actions

You may not consider swaying to a jazzed-up march very sensual. Let's go a step further, then, and transport our young man to the discotheque. How will he respond to the rhythm he hears now? No doubt about the music's control over the physical here. If we took him back to Mozart's day and the minuet his physical response would be quite different. It is the rhythm that controls the body's actions.

Dissonance Used Sparingly In Great Classics

Dissonance is a clashing of harmonies. Early composers used dissonance sparingly, always within a well defined framework of rules. Palestrina, Bach, Handel, Haydn and Mozart followed these rules faithfully. Later composers like Wagner, Mahler and Sibelius broadened this framework of dissonance in order to build dramatic effects and climaxes in their compositions. It was the musical spice. Just a dash here and there was all that was needed.

In our 20th century, however, dissonance has become so common that instead of the spice, it has often become the main dish. Noise and clatter have become a way of life, not only in music but in modern society in general. Hall states,

> "It is quite possible that the dissonance of our intensive, mechanized program of living are responsible, at least in part, for the rapid increase in nervous and psychoneurotic ailments."[1]

Dissonance Builds Tension

In order to be satisfying to our ears and to release bodily tensions, dissonance must resolve to consonance (more pleasing) harmony. Unresolved dissonances, which are so much a part of contemporary music, both serious and popular, are a factor in building tension and frustration. Listening to continued discord builds tension that calls for release, just as rhythm does. Unlike the response to rhythm, which is primarily in physical movement,

---

[1]Hall, op. cit., p. 17.

dissonance creates a mental and emotional restlessness. If you have attended concerts where the music of Stockhausen, Schonberg or John Cage has been played you will know the feeling.

C.P.E. Bach, (one of Johann Sebastian Bach's famous sons) set down these rules,

> *"Dissonances are played loudly and consonance softly, since the former rouse our emotions and the latter quiet them."*

Clashing harmonies possibly even more than repetitious rhythm can create nervous tension in an entire audience. Play a series of dissonant chords stopping short of the resolution for a group of musicians and watch them squirm. If someone were to strike an unresolved dissonance on the piano and walk away there would probably be a line-up at the piano to play the resolution. But the audience doesn't need to be made up of musicians. Even a non-musician will have the sensation of being left *"dangling"* until the chord resolves.

Rite of Spring ... Then And Now

Typical of 20th century composers and considered one of the giants of this generation was Igor Stravinski. Some of his music is filled with dissonance upon dissonance in seemingly unrelated patterns of sounds. (At least to the average listener it seems that way.) The first performance of his Rite of Spring was given in Paris in 1913. The audience, accustomed to the lyrical melodies and rich harmonies of Beethoven, Brahms, Schubert and even the impressionisms of Debussy, were not prepared for Stravinski. Angered by such an affront on their musical tastes, they booed, whistled, stomped and tossed assorted fruits and vegetables onto the stage. So great was the din and confusion through the entire performance that the conductor, Pierre Monteux, had difficulty hearing the orchestra he was conducting.

But today the Rite of Spring is standard repertoire with most symphony orchestras. Gone now are the catcalls and ripe tomatoes. Audiences will sit through the performance and applaud politely, if not enthusiastically, when it is finished. What has taken place since 1913 to change things? The music is still as harsh and dissonant as it was then. It is the listeners who have changed. Repeated exposure has created a tolerance. What was once harsh and unpleasant to the ear is now quite acceptable. Is this just a natural progression in the musical education of audiences? Partly. I, however, believe it is even more an indication that we have reached the saturation level of permissiveness in our society. We have learned to accept harshness in music and coarseness in art and literature as normal.

8
THAT'S ROCK

Today Rock-n-roll is being heard in Christian homes across the land. By merely adding religious words it also is suddenly transformed into the "*new*" church music.

* * *

According to a national survey, 87% of all teen-agers are exposed to rock music 3-5 hours a day. This includes Christian teens!

* * *

Rock is more than just music. It is the energy center of the new culture and youth revolution.

* * *

Rock music, more than any other previous form of popular music, is able to create mass hysteria and behavior changes in young people.

* * *

At rock concerts when the tempo of the music hits a certain pitch it brings a psychological response which the audience is powerless to resist.

8
THAT'S ROCK

Christian Young People Listen To Rock-n-roll

Thirty five years ago *"rock-n-roll music was only a gaudy sound in southern beer joints and on several hundred poorly waxed race records."*[1] Today, through some imaginary refining process, it is being heard in Christian homes across the land. By merely adding religious words it also is suddenly transformed into the *"new"* church music.

How many Christian young people are listening to rock? According to a national survey 87% of all teen-agers are exposed to rock music 3-5 hours a day. Does this include Christian teens? A private poll taken in the Wheaton, Illinois, area would seem to indicate that it does. Several hundred young people, ages 13-20, were interviewed about their musical preferences. More than half of those interviewed professed to be Christians (said they had received Christ as personal Savior), but there was little difference between their

---

[1] Ira Peck, ed. *The New Sound Yes* (Scholastic Book Services, 1966) p. 26.

musical tastes and those of the non-Christians. The majority of the boys preferred hard rock, the majority of the girls, soft rock.

What is rock? Is it just a harmless pop style that young people like to listen to? Or is it, as some say, a device of Satan's to gain control of the souls of this generation. Let's start at the beginning.

The scene is deep south U.S.A.

> There in the late 1930's in the fields and shanties of the delta country, evolved an earthy, hard-driving style of music called "rhythm and blues"—played by Blacks for Blacks. Cured in misery, it was a lonesome, soul-sad music full of cries and wails punctuated by a heavy, regular beat.[1]

How Rock-n-roll Got Its Name

In the early 1950's a Cleveland disc jockey, Alan Freed, was one of the first whites to play rhythm and blues over the air. He had borrowed the term, "rock-n-roll" (a ghetto expression sometimes used to mean illicit sex), and attached it to this music.

One of the first white groups to play the new music was Bill Haley and his Comets. He recorded, in 1951, Crazy Man Crazy which eventually sold a million copies. Two years later, Rock Around the Clock became his first big money maker. In 1954 an unknown black group, The Chords, cut Sh-Boom. In a short time it was number one in Los Angeles. The Crew Cuts, a

---

[1]Ira Peck, ed. *The New Sound Yes* (Scholastic Book Services, 1966) p. 4.

Elvis Presley became a victim of the Rock culture when he died of a drug overdose in 1977. Dr. George C. Nichopoulos, Presley's personal physician admitted that Elvis gobbled up vast amounts of drugs *". . . from the time he woke up in the morning until the time he went to sleep at night."*

white group, did a reissue of it shortly after and it became a national hit.

Teens Flip Over Elvis

Then, in 1956, a young southerner named Elvis Presley stepped before the cameras on a national telecast. With his hair flapping in his face, voice charged with emotion and hips gyrating, he wailed, *"Ah wa-ha-hunt yew-hoo, Ah nee-heed yew-hoo."* A new era was born. He sang and millions of teen-agers flipped. So did millions of parents. But for different reasons.

> *"He outraged adult sensibilities. But the more parents, moralists, clergymen and critics railed against him, the more teen-agers flipped for him. Elvis was, for them, the supreme symbol of juvenile rebellion."*[1]

Wherever Elvis went there were great crowds of young people. There were often riots—in Hartford, Atlanta, San Jose, Minneapolis, Boston and Washington. Theaters were demolished in London and Sao Paulo, Brazil. A storm of national protest grew. Church and civic leaders were soon insisting that rock-n-roll be banned. A senate subcommittee began investigating the link between rock music and juvenile delinquency. Frank Sinatra called the new music *"a rancid smelling aphrodisiac."* Jackie Gleason said it wouldn't last.[2] But it did!

---

[1]Ira Peck, ed. *The New Sound Yes* (Scholastic Book Services, 1966) p. 62.

[2]Gleason later offered Elvis a huge sum of money to appear on his program only to be turned down because it was below Presley's minimum.

Rock Performing Groups Come And Go

Soon there were groups of eager amateurs popping up to cash in on the growing popularity of rock-n-roll—and disappearing just as fast—Herman's Hermits, led by a 16-year-old high school drop-out, The Animals, The Honeycomers, the Ripchords, Bent Fabric, The Temptations, Goldie and the Gingerbreads and many more, came and went. Chubby Checkers, a one-time Philadelphia chicken plucker, danced into the musical spotlight and issued his invitation, *"C'mon baby, let's do the twist."* For the first time since the jitterbug, teen-agers had a new dance of their own. It became a national rage. Yet rock was still tossed off as a passing fad. Certainly it would eventually die out just as all the other musical fads had. The nation's parents plugged their ears and patiently waited.

Then came the Beatles, and the music that refused to go away turned the pop world upside down and created a national epidemic.

The Beatles Emerge As Teens' Heroes

The Beatles' appearance in February, 1964, on the Ed Sullivan Show was watched by an estimated 68,000,000 people, one of the largest TV audiences in history. As Elvis Presley had done eight years before, the Beatles—with their amplified music, long hair, undersized suits and high heeled boots—angered adults. Teen-agers flipped again. It was love at first sight.

The four young Englishmen from Liverpool, who had originally called themselves The Quarrymen Skiffle Group, had been, in the mid 1950's, only one of an estimated 100 rock-n-roll groups in the smog-aired dock-front city. They were discovered there by Brian Epstein, an ex-dress designer in charge of his father's television-radio-records department chain store. When he began to plug them, they soon had four hits. Mobs of teen-agers began following the Beatles wherever they went.

Rock Leads To Riches

The rest is history—the transcontinental tours, the sold-out performances, the riots and the decoration by Queen Elizabeth. In a short time the Beatles were international celebrities and millionaires. Their fan mail exceeded 12,000 letters a day. Income from personal appearances, record sales and royalties from other enterprises netted them $14,000,000 in 1964. Beatle wigs, Beatle T-shirts and a variety of other Beatle licensed products grossed over $50,000,000 in America alone the same year. In Liverpool, 60 teen-agers collapsed from exposure after standing all night in a mile-long line to get tickets for a *"back home again"* Beatle concert. When a foreman shut off the radio during a Beatle record at a textile mill in Lancashire 200 girls walked out on strike. And although they had stopped singing together many years ago ... their popularity still continues. Beatlemania, a musical extravaganza (which imitates the Beatles style), experiences sell-out crowds in the 1980 concerts.

Riding on the popularity of the Beatles, rock-n-roll was in.

"We are more popular than Jesus now."—John Lennon.

A memorable mansion

Former Beatle **John Lennon** has purchased an ocean-front mansion in Palm Beach, Fla., for $700,000, according to the Palm Beach socialite who sold the home.

Lennon and his wife, **Yoko Ono,** used the home on previous stays in Palm Beach. The palatial Spanish-style home has seven bedrooms, quarters for five servants, two swimming pools and 150 feet of beach front.

Lennon's fortune is said to include more than $150 million in real estate holdings and other investments from his money-making days in the 1960s as one of the Beatles.

Lennon Says Beatles Had Orgies and Dope

San Francisco — (UPI) — Former Beatle John Lennon says the rock music group indulged in sexual orgies on tours and made heavy use of drugs.

Despite this, he says, The Beatles managed to maintain a "clean image" for years.

The **Beatles** displaying their Order of the British Empire medals after Queen Elizabeth made the presentation in October, 1965. John Lennon of the Beatles once remarked: "Christianity will go. It will vanish and shrink. I needn't argue about that. I'm right and I will be proven right. We're more popular than Jesus now."

**Folk Music
Gives Way
To
Rock music**

So fast and so thoroughly did rock take the country that the simple folk music led by the Kingston Trio, The Brothers Four and The Chad Mitchell Trio that had held the number one spot since the mid 1950's quickly began to fade. The tidy, Ivy-league look of the folk groups gave way to the unkempt, faded jean hippy style dress of the new rock groups. The calm, melodious folk music sung to the accompaniment of acoustical guitars was replaced by the frenzied, hard driving, electrically amplified sound of rock music.

**Rock
Gives Voice
To A
Rebellious
Generation**

Bob Dylan, who had originally been a part of the folk scene, emerged as a leader in a new folk-rock style.* He was followed by the Byrds, Sonny and Cher, and Simon and Garfunkle. The folk singers had majored mostly in simple ballads like the Kingston Trio's *"Tom Dooley"* or *"The Green Leaves of Summer"* of The Brothers Four. Now the message was centered in anti-establishment themes—protest, violence, drugs and sex. Dylan's 1969 song *"Lay Lady Lay"* became a hit. The Rolling Stones contributed *"Let's Spend the Night Together"* and *"I Can't Get No Satisfaction,"* which sold 4.5 million copies. The Beatles offered *"Lucy in the Sky with Diamonds (LSD)"* and *"Yellow Submarine,"* which had obvious references to marijuana. Jefferson Airplane were singing *"Come all you Volunteers of America, You've got to Revolution."*

By the mid sixties 130,000,000 records

---

*In the mid 1970's, Dylan made a profession of Christ.

(90% of the total single records) were rock. Album sales added another 100,000,000. A decade later the rock music industry was to total almost 2 billion dollars a year.

Rock was here to stay. Yet it was obvious that it was more than just another harmless musical fad. Rock was the reflection of an age. It was a mood, a state of mind, a deep-seated rebellion against all that good society represented.

Counter-culture Grew Out Of Rock Music

In the 1960's secular journalists wrote of the new music:

> Rock . . . is an established pervasive social force and is still growing.[1]

> It's arrogant, aggressive, slaps you right in the face. Rock is the first music ever addressed directly to the teen-age world.[2]

Time magazine's issue for February 22, 1971, reported:

> The Counterculture sprang more than anything else from rock-n-roll music. The shattering, obliterating volume . . . amounted to a new form of violence . . . coupled with the anarchic, brute-sexual rhythm and lyrics of rock-n-roll music. The counterculture is the world's first socio-political movment to grow out of the force of electronically amp-lified music.

---

[1] John Rublowsky, *Popular Music* (Basic Books Inc. 1967) p. 14.
[2] Peck, p. 19.

The Rock magazine *Rolling Stone* added: "Rock is more than just music. It is the energy center of the new culture and youth revolution."

The Emotional Power Of Rock

The social implications of rock were frightening enough, but there was an even greater manifestation of the music's grip on teen-agers. For example, headlines in The Longbeach Independent of November, 1964, read: *"Police Close Frenzied Arena Show."* The article describes how a dozen policemen fought a valiant but losing battle with 5000 frenzied, screaming teen-age girls. The show, held in the Long Beach Arena, was halted before it was finished because of the hysterical crowd. *"Time and again, girls stormed the stage of the rock-n-roll concert given by The Pacemakers and Billy Jay Kramer."* Why did the girls make repeated attempts to fight their way to the stage? What were they intending to do once they got there? The spectacle of thousands of screaming girls charging the platform might be amusing—if it weren't so frightening. This is the power of rock.

Rock Concerts Become Scenes of Violence

Rock concerts all around the world were creating mass hysteria and violence.
- In Vancouver, during a 30 minute Beatles performance 100 people were *"stomped upon, gouged and assaulted."*
- In Melbourne nearly 1000 were injured at a rock concert.
- Fire hoses were needed to disperse hysterical fans in Beirut, Lebanon.
- A Rolling Stones concert in 1969 held in Altamont, California, drew more than

11 are killed in stampede at concert

Cincinnati rock event then goes on

Clothes lost in the crush: People were stacked up like kindling

Young people gathered outside Cincinnati's Riverfront Coliseum at 2 in the afternoon just 3 weeks before Christmas, 1979. This was 6 hours before the British rock group, **The Who,** were to appear. By 7:30 PM there were close to 7000 fans outside. When the doors opened a stampede occurred as young people rushed to get the best seats. When the chaos ended, 11 people were dead, crushed under the feet of the uncontrolled crowd!

300,000, creating huge traffic jams. The Hell's Angels were hired to *"police"* the event in which one person was killed and three others died of drug overdoses.

During the 60's and early 70's rock *"festivals"* were held all over the world. The total number of young people who attended these festivals, some running for several days, ran into the millions. When it became obvious these were nothing more than gigantic orgies they were outlawed in most places.

Rock Music Produces Mass Hysteria

Because rock, more than any other previous form of popular music, was able to create such mass hysteria and behavior changes in young people, worried authorities began seriously to investigate. Studies were made and reports compiled in hopes of finding a cause of the national teen-age monomania. Researchers, journalists and newspaper reporters began putting in personal appearances at rock concerts in order to get an inside view. Here is what one first hand spectator reported of *Sly and the Family Stone:*

> *After an hour or so, even I felt drugged. But 20,000 people, most of them high on marijuana, if nothing stronger, were rocking the whole building, swaying, standing on their seats, arms around each other . . . . The crowd seemed hypnotized in thrall. It was part of a mass frenzy. . . .*[1]

[1] Readers Digest, July 1973, p. 173.

**Rock
Compared
To
Voodoo Drums**

Rock has a heavy, incessant, throbbing beat, the same beat that people in primitive cultures use in their demonic rites and dances. If the beat is monotonous enough and the volume loud enough it can induce a type of hypnosis. Dr. Walter Wright, Ontario psychiatrist, in a report to the Candian Association of Music Therapy (*Calgary Herald*, May 19, 1976),

compared rock to voodoo drums:

> *The tempo of the voodoo drums has been known to make a listener powerless to resist the music's pounding beat .. . . At rock concerts when the tempo of the music hits a certain pitch it brings a psychological response which the audience is powerless to resist.*

Jeremy Larner, writing in *The New Sound, Yes,* states,

> *When a listener submits himself to the beat, he loosens his mind from its moorings in space and time . . . The difficult world of external objects is blurred and unreal; only the inner pulse is real, the beat its outer projection. Earthly worries are submerged in a rising tide of exultation.*[1]

And this is the opinion of Mike Quatro, well-known producer of rock shows:

> *Rock motivates you internally, gives you a sensual feeling. A girl can be turned on by the music. It releases her inhibitions. The beat of the drum has always been a factor . . . A girl realizes her own sexuality through the music.*[1]

This chapter may not have given encouragment to the teen who enjoys this music.

But that's rock!

---

[1]Peck, op. cit., p. 112.

At the request of *The Seattle Times* Dr. Bernard Saibel, child guidance expert for the Washington State Division of Community Services, attended a concert of the Beatles. After the performance he wrote:

> *The experience of being with 14,000 teen-agers to see the Beatles is unbelievable and frightening . . . . The hysteria and loss of control go far beyond the impact of the music. Many of those present became frantic, hostile, uncontrolled, screaming, unrecognizable beings. . . . This is not simply a release, as I first thought it would be, but a very destructive process.*
>
> *Normally recognizable girls behaved as possessed by some demonic urge, defying in emotional ecstasy the restraints which authorities try to place on them.*[1]

"Frenzy"—"hysteria"—"hostile"— "demonic." What was it all about? What was the cause of it?

The music!

---

[1] The Seattle Times, August 22, 1964, p. 1.

9

SIDE EFFECTS . . . THE ULTIMATE PENALTY

A steady diet of Rock-n-roll junk promotes degenerate rebelliousness among teen-agers that finds its outlet in drugs, alcohol and illicit sex.

* * *

A California music therapist, investigating the effects of rock music on teen-agers, administered an emotional stability test. The results were then examined by a psychologist (who was unaware of the experiment). His conclusions were astounding!

* * *

The Beatles admitted, *"Our music is capable of causing emotional instability, disorganized behavior, rebellion and even revolution."*

* * *

Rock music is a pollutant every bit as deadly as pornography. Rock, with its almost total emphasis on the beat, bypasses the mind and works directly on the body.

9

SIDE EFFECTS ... THE ULTIMATE PENALTY!

**Rock Music
A Cause
Of Youth
Problems**

From its beginnings and throughout its 25 year history, rock has had a negative influence on the lives of its young listeners. While the tremendous increase in teenage pregnancies, venereal diseases, problems in schools and rebelliousness cannot *all* be traced to rock music, there is rising evidence that there is a relationship between the music and the ills of the nation's youth.

Today, the corporate voice of Christians, which should be letting out a mightly wail against rock music, is emitting a mere peep; whereas the secular world has taken the reins and is beginning to speak out in concern.

•Gene Lees, writing in the February 1970 issue of *High Fidelity*, warned:

If you ask me whether rock music has been a symptom or a cause of America's terrible problems with its young people, I would be inclined to say both—but primarily a cause.

Rock Music And Crime

- In 1974, one of my former students was employed as a secretary in the juvenile division of the Calgary police department. Since, at the time, I was gathering material for a lecture which later became the basis for this book, I was happy to have the contact that would allow me the opportunity to gain some valuable information. Was there any correlation between listening to rock music and crimes committed by juveniles booked into the station?

Of the 25 officers, detectives and others interviewed who handled these cases, 23 believed that there was some, if not great, influence of the music on the youthful offenders. One officer stated that he believed rock music was a major influence in a murder.

- In 1977, the Population Institute of San Francisco was alarmed by the epidemic of teen-age pregnancies. Many believed that such explicit songs as *"You're Having My Baby," "Let's Spend the Night Together,"* and *"Afternoon Delight"* were to blame. So the Population Institute decided to take action. The result was Rock Project, in which 35 top singing stars were enlisted to take to the air with *"don't get pregnant"* messages.

**Rock-n-roll
A Legalized
Racket**

How well these "counter messages" worked is not known.

- Columnist Phyllis Schlafly tells of a letter she received from professional musician Jack Staulcup in response to an article she had written deploring the sex rock trend. She wrote in 1978:

> According to Staulcup, a steady diet of rock and roll junk promotes degenerate rebelliousness among teen-agers that finds its outlet in drugs, alcohol and illicit sex.
>
> . . . It is strange that government and public interest groups which have been so concerned about air, water and land pollution, never utter a word about ear, mind or moral pollution . . .
>
> Staulcup concludes that rock and roll is the biggest legalized racket this country has ever seen. If we value civilization, we cannot afford to ignore any longer the high correlation between the multibillion dollar hard rock racket and the explosion of drug use and illicit sex among their teenage victims.
>
> Parents should take a more active part in monitoring their children's entertainment.[1]

- In 1978, a California music therapist, investigating the effects of rock music on teen-agers, administered to 240 school children aged 10-18 an emo-

---

[1]The Olean (N.Y.) *Times Herald*, 1978, p. 18.

tional stability test during which rock was being played.

The results were then examined by a psychologist who was unaware of the experiment. He concluded that the test had been given in a mental institution.

This same therapist also found that in tests using an auto-driver trainer simulating actual driving conditions, that listening to rock while behind the wheel increased the incidence of driver's error by 34.4%.

A Deaf Generation

• From a physical standpoint there is plenty of evidence that the loud blare of rock has left a generation of young people hard of hearing. In the mid 60's colleges were finding that the average entering freshman possessed only the hearing efficiency of a typical 65-year-old.

In experiments with guinea pigs, the unfortunate rodents, too, developed hearing problems when exposed to rock for comparable lengths of time and at similar decibel levels as these young people would be listening.

But it is the rock musicians and promoters themselves who provide the clincher. There has never been any doubt in their minds about the effect of the music on the lives of teen-agers.

What Rock Musicians Admit

Here are the views expressed by some of them:

The Beatles (in the late 60's):

Our music is capable of causing emotional instability, disorganized be-

havior, rebellion and even revolution.

Spencer Dryden:

Get them while they're young. Bend their minds.

Jan Berry:

The throbbing beat of rock provides a vital sexual release for its adolescent audience.

Andrew Oldham (recording manager of the Rolling Stones):

Pop music is sex and you have to hit them in the face with it.

Donnie Brewer of Grand Funk:

We take the kids away from their parents and their environment to where the only reality is the rhythm and the beat.

John Denver . . . though primarily a folk and country-Western singer, says of rock:

Rock music is a greater influence over the souls of men than primitive Christianity.

These statements should ring loud and clear to Christians.

Sex-Oriented Lyrics

Parents of teens who listen to rock should be aware of what it is their sons and daughters are being fed. The sex-oriented lyrics combined with the sensual rhythm of the music can only lead the young listener down the road to carnality. The familiar rationalization, *"But I don't listen* to the words, only the music," has always been a little on the incredible side. One doesn't buy a record or a tape and play it once. Repeated playings will saturate the mind with both the message of the words and the meaning of the music.

Rock Is A Kind Of Pornography

Rock music is a pollutant every bit as deadly as pornography. Pornography takes what God has created good and pure and changes it into something with the sole purpose of satisfying our lustful appetites. Good music, with its balance of melody, harmony and rhythm has its appeal to the mind and intellect. Rock, with its almost total emphasis on the beat bypasses the mind and works directly on the body.

Can you imagine this conversation?

What do you have there, son?
Just a copy of Playboy, Dad.
Oh. Well, if you're going to look at that, go into your room and shut the door where we can't see you.
O.K. Dad. Sure will.

Problem solved? Obviously not. The dialogue would more likely go like this!

You throw that corruption in the garbage where it belongs, and don't you ever bring anything like that in here again!

Yes, Dad.

But in many Christian homes the record and tape collection of this musical corruption continues to grow with little regulation by Mom and Dad. Parents' only reaction often is, *"If you're going to listen to that, go in your room and shut the door so we can't hear it."*

Why? For the simple reason that we do not recognize rock as pornographic. Christians who would gasp in horror at the thought of adorning their living room wall with lewd pictures or having offensive literature lying on the reading table are allowing their children to enjoy the lust of the flesh via a spinning turntable.

The influence of rock music unchecked by a nation of confused parents could very well be a major factor in the moral and spiritual decline of a generation of young people.

MUSICAL INFLUENCES

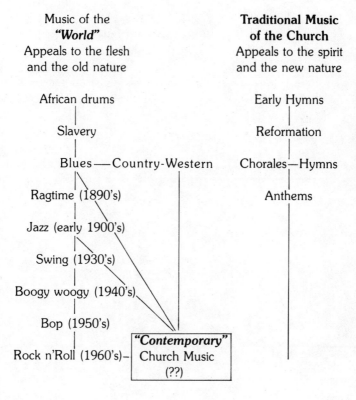

Music of the *"World"* Appeals to the flesh and the old nature	Traditional Music of the Church Appeals to the spirit and the new nature
African drums	Early Hymns
Slavery	Reformation
Blues — Country-Western	Chorales — Hymns
Ragtime (1890's)	Anthems
Jazz (early 1900's)	
Swing (1930's)	
Boogy woogy (1940's)	
Bop (1950's)	
Rock n'Roll (1960's) — *"Contemporary"* Church Music (??)	

The *"new"* Christian music has its origins in the world not in the traditional music of the church.

10

STRANGE MUSIC TO THEIR EARS

No matter how doctrinally sound the words are, rock, by its nature, can never be used to communicate spiritual truth. Not hard rock, not soft rock. Not any kind of rock. Rock music and godly things just don't go together.

* * *

The Bible condemns the combining of the holy with the unholy. 2 Corinthians 6:14 warns us of this. Rock is evil. Using rock to communicate with young people is conforming to the world. And it is wrong!

* * *

It is not possible to use the same music in one part of the world for the devil's service while using it for God in another.

* * *

Why are we so star struck? Why do we idolize Christian singers and speakers? We spend more money on gospel records and concerts than we give to worthy missions!

10

STRANGE MUSIC TO THEIR EARS

**A Pig
Is Still
A Pig**

Now let's lift rock music out of the pop culture, out of the discotheques and night clubs, and replace all the offensive words with Christian words. Let's bring it into the church, have Christian people perform it and call it *"Christian"* rock. Does it now become Christianized? **No!**

To illustrate: Suppose you have invited a friend over for dinner. But at the last minute he calls and can't make it. There sits that delectable meal on the table. You don't want to eat alone. What to do? Flash, an idea. You go outside and down the path to the pig pen. There sits old Mortimer, wallowing in the mud. *"Well, Mort,*

I guess you'll have to do." You take Mortimer out of the pen, scrub him off and give him a good hosing. Then you bring him into the house, dress him in a suit and plunk him down beside you at the table. There he sits in his nice suit, clean shirt and tie. He's not much to look at. But at least he smells better—and he's company. There is only one thing wrong. He's still a pig, and he will continue to act like one at the table.

It's the same with rock music. You can dress it up and try to make it respectable. You can even title it *"Christian."* But underneath it is still the same sensuous, neurotic music that it always was. It is still capable of creating in the listener the same attitudes and traits that it represents.

Let's look at it another way. Suppose you are standing on a street corner. A drunk comes staggering down the mall. He's filthy. He's ragged. He reeks of alcohol. He comes wobbling up to you and says, *"Praise the Lord. Jesus has transformed me."* Then he begins to quote Scripture.

Rock Cannot Communicate Spiritual Truth

What would be your reaction? Would you believe him? Would you put your arm on his shoulder and say, *"Well, bless you, brother, it's good to have fellowship with you."* Probably not. You might feel more like telling him to move on. Why? What would be wrong? There was nothing wrong with what he said. He was quoting Scripture. But it was the filthy condition of the person who said those words that repulsed you.

The first arrivals came on Monday, even though the festival wasn't scheduled to begin until Friday. The early ones were hard-core hippies, used to being on the road. They set up camp and waited for the "plastic hippies," the middle-class teen-agers who would arrive later in the week.

From the start, the two most striking phenomena at Powder Ridge, as at all festivals, were costumes and drugs. The costumes hit your eye first. They recalled a huge, disorganized Halloween party: gaudy tank tops and tie-dyed T-shirts; beaded, fringed, and festooned shirts and jackets; tight-fitting jeans and ballooning granny dresses; see-through blouses and, occasionally, no blouses at all. The attitude toward nudity was nonchalant and matter-of-fact.

Then there were the drugs. The pushers arrived early and set up shop openly, with crudely printed signs or banners proclaiming their wares. Many sat chanting out their offerings:

"Mescaline, $1 a trip."

The Big Turn-On

Then there were the drugs. The pushers arrived early and set up shop openly, with crudely printed signs or banners proclaiming their wares. Many sat chanting out their offerings:

"Mescaline, $1 a trip."

"LSD, 75 cents for a four-way tab" (a tablet that could be broken into four parts for separate trips).

"Grass, $8 a lid" (about an ounce of marijuana, good for seven or eight cigarettes).

Hashish, amphetamines, the whole turn-on catalog was available.

Almost everyone used marijuana, the youngsters from respectable homes and the real hippies alike. I would guess that at least nine of every 10 young people there smoked grass. Usually, the joints were passed around. Sharing marijuana is an act of hospitality in the drug world.

Another reason for drug use is equally ancient—the pressure to do something because everyone else is doing it. When a young person is in a crowd of his friends who are smoking grass, he'll join in because he doesn't want to be called chicken. "When all your friends are high and you're not, you're out of it," one girl explained. Said another teen-ager: "Just as long as you know you're stoned, you know you're with it." Like all young people, this generation wants to be with it, even when there are heavy risks involved.

In **Family Health** magazine, a youth expert reports on the rock festival phenomenon and its drug culture that seduces the young.

The court injunction that prevented the Powder Ridge Music Festival from being held in Middlefield, Connecticut, helped turn it into a week-long drug festival for many of the 30,000 people—mostly kids, but with a sprinkling of young family groups—who arrived in search of a Woodstock-like celebration of life. Hand-lettered signs told the story. Where drugs were concerned, anything went. Sales were brisk and out in the open. One LSD dealer, with cash on his lap (*below*), gave free samples to prove he was selling "the real thing."

Plentiful supplies of drugs produced a price war. The cost of an LSD trip was as low as 75 cents. Even so, there was ample profit for the sellers. One of the very few drug pushers who were arrested carried $13,000 in bills.

For physicians manning the makeshift hospital in a tent, Powder Ridge was a truly bad scene. They treated nearly 1,000 severe drug reactions, many caused by uninhibited experimentation that produced bizarre combinations such as LSD laced with strychnine "for a faster, groovier high."

For many, Powder Ridge turns into a bad trip

The court injunction that prevented the Powder Ridge Music Festival from being held in Middlefield, Connecticut, helped turn it into a week-long drug festival for many of the 30,000 people—mostly kids, but with a sprinkling of young family groups—who arrived in search of a Woodstock-like celebration of life. Hand-lettered signs told the story. Where drugs were concerned, anything went. Sales were brisk and out in the open. One LSD dealer, with cash on his lap (*below*), gave free samples to prove he was selling "the real thing."
Plentiful supplies of drugs produced a price war. The cost of an LSD trip was as low as 75 cents. Even so, there was ample profit for the sellers. One of the very few drug pushers who were arrested carried $13,000 in bills.
For physicians manning the makeshift hospital in a tent, Powder Ridge was a truly bad scene. They treated nearly 1,000 severe drug reactions, many caused by uninhibited experimentation that produced bizarre combinations such as LSD laced with strychnine "for a faster, groovier high." When the last exhausted straggler left, Powder Ridge looked more like a battlefield than a festival of life.

This same rock-oriented music has now infiltrated Christian circles. When Satan can't lick them ... he joins them masquerading as an angel of light deviously detouring the faithful and watering down their effectiveness for the Lord Jesus Christ.

**Rock
Cannot
Communicate
Spiritual
Truth**

We should be repulsed too when we hear God's Word accompanied by the racy sound of rock. No matter how doctrinally sound the words are, rock, by its nature, can never be used to communicate spiritual truth. Not hard rock. Not soft rock. Not any kind of rock. Rock music and godly things just don't go together.

There are many well-meaning Christians who say that they do. To prove it they point to all the *"good results"* with teenagers when rock is used to communicate the gospel to them. But wait a minute! Does this practice line up with Scripture?

No, it doesn't. The Bible condemns the combining of the holy with the unholy. 2 Corinthians 6:14 warns us not to be *"unequally yoked together with unbelievers."* In principle this would certainly apply to yoking the holy words of Scripture with the sensual sound of rock. In verse 17 of the same chapter we are commanded to *"Come out from among them and to touch not the unclean thing."* Is rock unclean? If we are to believe the statements of rock performers it is. We are also exhorted to abstain from the appearance of evil (1 Thessalonians 5:22). Is rock evil? Yes. We are not to be conformed to the world (Romans 12:2). Is using rock to communicate with young people conforming to the world? Yes.

**Demonic
Music**

The folly of putting Christian lyrics to rock was brought home by an incident related to me by Doug, one of my former students. Doug's parents, Elmer and Ruth Warkentin, serve as missionaries in Kalimantan. One day his sister Jan received a visitor who had flown in from the United States. Jan's friend had brought along some of the latest Christian contemporary albums. The walls of Kalimantan homes are not noted for their "soundproofness," and as one of these songs was being played in the living room, the music floated out into the street. Some members of the local congregation happened to be walking by and heard the strange sound coming from the missionary's house. Wide-eyed and bewildered, they rushed to the house and asked excitedly, "Why are you calling on the spirits with your music?" They had no way of knowing that what they were hearing was not the music of the medicine man, but merely the latest "Christian" music from America. To them this music meant only that the missionary had left his senses and was communicating with demons.

An Experience Related

Months later Doug shared a portion of a letter with me which he had received from another sister, Ellen. She was attending a well-known Christian college when she related this experience:

> Last night was weird! I woke up at about 12:30 because I was talking in my sleep. I had said rather firmly,
> And in Jesus' name, amen.
>
> My dream had been about some Satanic attack and I was pleading the blood of Jesus. Then because the attack was so strong, I had said, And in Jesus' name, amen.

There was such a tension—I was nearly trembling. The hair on my arms was standing up. Then I realized why. The room next to me had on some rock music and the beat was exactly like that of a **belinggang** [*a Dyak word for the beat the witchdoctor uses in his demonic rites.*] I woke them up and asked them to turn it off. Then I slept so peacefully—and even slept in.

Is it possible to use the same music in one part of the world for the devil's service while using it for God in another? The answer must be a resounding, No!

Why are Christians Involved In Rock?

In spite of illustrations like this and clear Biblical injunctions against mixing holiness with unholiness, Christian people (both youth and adult) continue to promote and listen to this music.

The reasons? Popularity. Fame. Money. A desire to be entertained . . . all hidden beneath the cloak called communication. To be sure, there are earnest individuals who, because of a lack of spiritual perception, have involved themselves in a "*contemporary music ministry.*" **But they, when presented with the truth, soon change their minds and music.**

Misplaced Priorities

In a discerning article, Music or Missions? (Firewind, Sept. 1978) Keith Green, himself a young singer in the Jesus rock movement, decries this situation. Beginning with a statement that he frequently has young people come to him wanting to know how they can get started in a music ministry, he writes an open letter to them. Here it is in part:

Why are we so star struck? Why do we idolize Christian singers and speakers? We go from glorifying Elton John in the world . . . to Andre Crouch when we become Christians. It's all idolatry!! Can't you see that??? . . . How come no one idolizes the missionaries who give up everything and live in poverty, endangering their lives and their families. . . . How come no one lifts up and exalts the ghetto and prison ministers. . . . How come??? Because (1) we're taught from very early on, that comfort is our goal and security . . . and (2) that we should always seek for a lot of people to like us!

Who lives more comfortably and has more 'fans' than the latest bright and shining gospel star? Who lives less comfortably and has less friends and supporters than selfless missionaries?

Why do you spend more money on gospel records and concerts than you give to World Vision to feed the poor, or to the missionaries your church is supporting?

Let's all repent of idolatry and seeking a comfortable 'rewarding' life while we are passing through like strangers and pilgrims in this world (Hebrews 11:13). Our due service to the Lord is 'not only to believe on

> Him, but also to suffer for His sake
> (Philippians 1:29)' . . .

A great chorus of amens is heard from Christian adults.

When the last amen has faded to an echo these questions may be asked: Who has allowed these young people to make idols of Christian musicians and to spend more money on albums than for missions? Who is producing this beguiling music for them to listen to?

11

THE OLD NEW SOUND

We are using the world's music as the basis for many of our new Christian songs.

* * *

The drift towards the world's music is evident even in the *"styling"* instructions of some of the new songs. This is typical of the contemporary Christian music approach today.

* * *

The world is not going to be fooled by our *"new"* Christian music. There is no difference. Brothels, bars, slums, sex, rebellion . . . this is the heritage of our Now Sound Christian music!

* * *

It is evident that some teen-agers are not being taught a respect for the authority of God's Word and therefore are not familiar enough with it to use it as a guide in everyday situations that call for decisions—in music or in other areas.

THE OLD NEW SOUND

Defining
"Contemporary"

How are rock and pop music in general influencing our Christian music today? When we talk about contemporary music or the new sound we are talking more about a style than about when it was written. Webster defines *contemporary* simply as *"existing or occurring at the same time."* This has no connotation one way or another. It is neither good nor bad. It is just something that is happening now.

Contemporary
Music
Not
Contemporary

But much of our church music that is called contemporary is not contemporary at all. It has been borrowed from musical styles that have been in existence since the late 1890's, when ragtime, grandfather of all "beat" music, became popular. But these styles—jazz coming before World War I, swing in the 1930's, boogie woogie in the 1940's, and rock in the 50's—have always been a part of the honky-tonk, ballroom, night club culture. They have never been a part of the church. Not until the youth revolution of the 60's did someone decide that this music would be just the thing to attract unsaved young people to Christ.

In short, we are using the world's music as the basis for many of our new Christian songs. In talking with many young people I find that they do not see this as wrong. To them there is no conflict at all in presenting spiritual truths draped in whatever attire unregenerate people will find acceptable. They do not understand that this is contrary to clear Biblical teaching. It is evident that these same teen-agers are not being taught a respect for the authority of God's Word and therefore are not familiar enough with it to use it as a guide in everyday situations that call for decisions—in music or in other areas. All the blame for the lack of spiritual discernment cannot be laid at young people's feet. A portion of the blame for this, at least, must be placed on the parents, the pastors, the youth leaders—those of us who are in positions of authority and leadership. We cannot pass on precepts to others that we ourselves have not learned. In Ezekiel 22:26 we find the same indictment placed against the Israelite leaders:

Who Is To Blame?

> Her priests have violated my law, and have profaned my holy things: they have put no difference between the holy and profane, neither have they shewed difference between the unclean and the clean. . . .

What a description of the situation we face today!

4 Students Shot to Death In Violence at Kent State

A coed screams and a student lies dead at Kent State University. He was one of four felled by bullets during clash of Ohio National Guardsmen with students protesting U. S. intervention in Cambodia.

Protesters Fired On By Guard

KENT, O., May 4 (UPI). —Four students were shot to death on the Kent State University campus Monday when National Guardsmen, claiming they were a sniper, fired on a group of young persons demonstrating against, extension of the Indochina war.

Map on Page 10

At least 11 other students were wounded in the brief volley of gunfire which crackled along the tree-lined campus shortly before noon.

The head of Ohio's National Guard and students differed in their versions of how the shooting began.

In Columbus, S. T. Del Corso, the sixth adjutant general, said that "a sniper opened fire against the Guardsmen from a nearby rooftop."

NO WARNING

Brig. Gen. Robert Canterbury, the commander of Guard troops on the campus, said no warning was given to the students that the troops would shoot.

Student eyewitnesses said they heard no gunfire until some of the Guardsmen began shooting. They said the Guardsmen at the time were retreating under a shower of rocks thrown by the demonstrators.

"All of a sudden," said one male student, "some of them turned around, faced the crowd of students and started firing."

The early 1970's were marked with protests by young people. Rock music kept the anger boiling and erupting in tragedy.

**What Rock
Producers
Say**

That the contemporary sound imitates worldly styles there is little argument. Here is what some of the musicians, and those who produce this music say about their own styles:

From a music specialist with Campus Life:

> My music is a combination of the many influences on my musical tastes—black gospel, semi-jazz, with a little rock thrown in.

From promotional copy describing various new albums:

- Ranging from a Chicago [Rock-Jazz group] sounding, My Tribute, to the country gospel music of Since I Opened the Door. . . .
- This recording combines the easy listening of Give Them All with the country-flavored soft rock of You Got the Power and includes a popular tune, For Baby.
- You'll be thrilled by Randie's interpretation of the hymn tune Amazing Grace covering styles from Bach to Elton John.
- These songs vary from rhythm and blues to tender ballads.
- The new album will use the same unique combination of rock, pop and country sounds . . . that first brought him national attention.

**New
Tempo
Markings**

The drift toward the world's music is evident even in the "styling" instructions of some of the new songs. Here, taken at random from a pile of new music on my desk, are some samples. In place of traditional tempo markings like *andante, allegro, moderato* are:

> *Very rhythmical*
> *Rock beat*
> *Driving*
> *Aggressive and Lively*
> *Bossa Nova*
> *Medium bounce*

Rock, rhythm and blues, jazz, pop tunes, Bossa Nova, etc. are all products of the world. These musicians are taking the sensual and the fleshly and are saying, in effect, *"We are going to appeal to the spiritual."* It cannot be done. It is neither logical nor scriptural. This is typical of the contemporary Christian music approach today. It is interesting to note that most of these styles have had their origin as dance music.

The Secular Viewpoint

Since the musicians themselves have freely used these secular styles and often with the purported purpose of reaching the world, let's see how the world views these styles. Taken from secular sources. . . . About jazz:

> The importance of jazz as a contribution to modern music is a greatly debated question. . . . Jazz is, of course, a stimulus coming from primitive art.
> Karl Nef
> *An Outline of the History of Music*

> Jazz to the pagan is the symptom of a glorious release from the bonds of

moral restraint . . . It came from the slums of music; it corrupted taste and manners.

Issa Goldberg, *Tinpan Alley*

About blues:

Blues, the lament of a lonely man or woman, were the outgrowth of the earlier sorrow songs in which the Negro race bewailed its sad fate.

Panorama of American Pop Music

The blues are songs of man's troubles and weariness, his problems with love and the law or inhumanity. They arose spontaneously as folk music of the Negro slaves in the south, though the rhythms have roots in Africa. The blues spread from workgangs and guitar playing slum troubadors to pianists in brothels and bars."

Encyclopedia of Popular Music

The World Is Not Fooled

These statements coming from secular writers, combined with what rock performers have said about their own music, indicate that the world is not going to be fooled by our "new" Christian music. There is no difference. It's just like theirs. Brothels, bars, slums, sex, rebellion. This is the heritage of our Now Sound Christian music!

12
SERVING GOD OR SATAN

Worldly music can be identified by its close associations with the world. The world's music is performed in night clubs, theaters or wherever unregenerate people gather to be entertained.

* * *

Worldly music can be identified by its sound. It employs the use of the *"scoop," "flip," "slump,"* delayed vibrato and several other vocal devices.

* * *

Popular songs center around earthy themes and the delivery, rhythmically and electronically is geared to achieve this purpose.

* * *

Instrumentally, there is a heavy emphasis on rhythm using the drums and bass guitar. Generally, there is a never-changing throbbing syncopation. You will recognize the dissonances and rhythms that keep the nervous system keyed up and tense.

12

SERVING GOD OR SATAN

**Worldliness
In
Music**

Now we come to the focal point in our evaluation of contemporary Christian music. The Bible emphasizes that though we as Christians are **in** the world we are not **of** the world (John 15:19), we are to be separated from it (2 Corinthians 6:17) and unspotted from it (James 1:27). We usually think of worldliness in terms of smoking, drinking, dancing, attending movies and other fleshly pleasures (or we used to). But what is worldliness in music? If worldly music is being used as the basis of our contemporary church music, then it is contrary to the Word of God.

**Satan's
Trojan
Horse**

But how can we be sure that it is or is not the world's music? How can we identify it? We are not now speaking of the words. Obviously words can promote Satan's world system philosophies. But how can melody, harmony and rhythm be considered worldly? This is more difficult to define. That's why I believe Satan has chosen music as his Trojan Horse.

Many supporters of the Now Sound, in order to justify the use of pop-style music in the church, argue that music itself is amoral—that it is neither good nor bad —and therefore communicates no message of its own. Its message, they say, is only the message of the words attached to it.

The argument is questionable. It was the beautiful sounds of David's harp that brought peace to Saul. It was Chopin's piano playing that calmed the Polish Governor's seizures. It was also the music that caused young people to riot and go into hysterics at rock concerts. It was music alone that controlled the actions of the African tribe in the missionary's experiment. It is music that helps mental patients to be cured of their neuroses. And whatever can control the behavior of individuals or groups of people for good or for bad is a moral force.

**Music
A
Moral Issue**

Dr. Howard Hanson, former director of the Eastman School of Music, once made this statement: "[Music] can be soothing or invigorating, ennobling or vulgarizing, philosophical or orgiastic. It has powers for evil as well as good."[1]

There seems to be little doubt that music, by itself, can have moral qualities. The type of music, then, that we use as a vehi-

[1]Howard Hanson, "A Musician's Point of View Toward Emotional Expression," American Journal of Psychiatry SC (1943), p. 317 . . . quoted by Frank Garlock, The Big Beat, A Rock Blast, (Bob Jones University Press, 1971), p. 44.

cle to communicate spiritual truths is important. Whatever style we use must, in its basic structure, be positive rather than negative. This would eliminate copying the sensual sounds of the world.

Trying to define something as elusive as worldly music is climbing out on a long limb. There are many shades and variables to be considered. But I believe it can be defined, and defined so that it is possible to recognize it without the aid of a degree in music.

Worldly Associations

First, worldly music can be identified by its close associations with the world.

The world's music is performed in night clubs, ball rooms, theaters or wherever unregenerate people gather to be entertained. Why do night club patrons prefer a certain type of music as they dance, sip their drinks or watch the floor show? Because it goes with what they are doing. It creates an atmosphere in which they can feel comfortable.

What would be their reaction if, one evening, the master of ceremonies announced,

> Tonight, ladies and gentlemen, we have something a little different for you. In place of our regular show, the band is going to play some of John Philip Sousa's most famous marches. O.K. boys, let's hear it!

Marches? Well, that might be all right for a novelty, as long as it happened only once every 85 years. But marches in a night club? Ugh!

Or how would the audience respond if the emcee stepped in front of the mike and exclaimed,

> Folks, we have a surprise. Tonight we're going to have an old-fashioned hymn sing.

The place would be deserted in a hurry. Or they would throw the emcee out the back door and continue on with what they had been listening to.

What kind of music do they want? Music with flesh appeal. Music that feeds the senses: Pop music. Marches, hymns and other forms of high class music just don't fit in with the earthy atmosphere of the night club, or other places of self-indulgent entertainment. On the other hand, romantic love ballads, blues, show tunes, rock and jazz do fit because they are flesh pleasers.

Worldly Sound

Second, worldly music can be identified by its sound.

Open in front of me is a book entitled, How to Sing for Money, published in 1939.[1] It was a *"how to do it"* guide for someone who was hoping to make the grade in the popular music field. Although it is now probably only a collector's item, it is still up-to-date in many of its technical suggestions for developing a *"hit style"* delivery. These are ideas and techniques that have been the stock-in-trade of two generations of pop singers, from Bing Crosby to Olivia Newton-John.

[1]Charles Henderson. (George Palmer Putnam, Inc., Hollywood).

In the late 1970's, **Alice Cooper** (whose real name is Vince Furnier), was a popular Rock star. For 90 minutes he would perform with black humor, sometimes dancing with a snake. His father and grandfather were ministers but Cooper had a vague concept of God. Alcohol almost ruined him until he spent 3 months in an institution for emotional rehabilitation in White Plains, New York. Now his greatest addiction is television. He has 22 sets in his house, located in every room. He never turns them off!

From a chapter on *Dynamics and Vocal Mannerisms*, the author, Charles Henderson, well-known arranger and vocal coach of the 30's, writes,

> There are certain effects which, though not strictly "natural," have an accepted use in popular singing.[1]

Then he describes the use of the *"scoop," "flip," "slump,"* delayed vibrato and several other vocal devices. He goes on to explain why these techniques are used:

> Haven't you heard, all too often, renditions which seemed to be technically correct in every detail—diction, phrasing, pace, stressing, everything right—but still something vaguely wrong somewhere? ... Often it is undue "swank." ... The trained singer's rendition of a simple little ballad, or rhythm song is often just plain <u>too good</u>. The tone quality is too rich, the air too cultured and the net effect is one of pompous churchy ostentation. The listeners are actually embarrassed. The public wants to feel a song not admire it.[2]

"Don't Be Too Good"

I am reminded of one shining example that illustrates Henderson's *"don't be too good"* advice. It happened many years ago on Your Hit Parade. For several weeks the nation's number one hit tune was a cowboy lament, *"Don't Fence Me*

[1] Charles Henderson, (George Palmer Putnam, Inc., Hollywood) p. 135.
[2] Ibid., p. 139.

In." Week after week Hit Parade listeners were treated to the strange sound of fading opera star, Lawrence Tibbett (evidently trying to keep the last ember from dying out), singing the song. But try as he would, he could not sing in the croony, sentimental style that was required to put the song across. Mr. Tibbett called upon his many years of vocal training and operatic experience and gave it all he had. But *"Don't Fence Me In"* still came out like an aria from Rigoletto. Though his voice still carried much of its former power and richness, he failed as a pop vocalist because, as Mr. Henderson cautions his hopeful pupils, *"the too good rendition is the prime pitfall in the path of the trained singer."*[1]

Techniques In Pop Singing

Let's be specific now and list some of the techniques mentioned in How to Sing for Money together with others used by most modern pop singers and performers. Remember, the aim of popular music is to give the listeners the right feeling, to create the right atmosphere. The rich, cultured delivery is to be avoided. The effect produced will be more important than the music. Since pop songs center around earthy themes the delivery will be of the same character.

*This is the characteristic sound of popular music.

---

[1]Charles Henderson, (George Palmer Putnam, Inc., Hollywood) p. 139.

*Listen to the top forty on radio anytime and you will hear "The Now Sound."

Melodically (vocal delivery)	Airy, limpid tone. Scooping and sliding from note to note. If played on instruments, imitates scoop and slide of voice. The scoop and slide is the essence of blues, which had its origins in the weeping and wailing of the black slaves.
Harmonically	Many unresolved dissonances: 6ths, 7ths, 9ths. Repetitive used of the same few chords.
Rhythmically	Never-changing throbbing syncopation. Often two or three syncopated rhythms played simultaneously. Heavy beat. You will recognize that the dissonances and rhythms are the same elements that keep the nervous system keyed up and tense.
Instrumentally	Heavy emphasis on rhythm instruments—drums and bass guitar. Until the inclusion of drums in the dance orchestra around the turn of the century in Western culture they were used primarily to help keep marchers in step. A modern combo of as few as three or four often uses a trap set (bass drum, snare, tom-toms, two cymbals) as well as bass guitar. Compare this with a symphony orchestra of 90 musicians that may use only one percussion instrument, the timpani, and this only sparingly.
Electronically	Almost total dependence upon a sound system, emphasizing even more the thump of the rhythm instruments. Alleviates, for the singer, the necessity of developing good vocalist production. Creates a *"mike in mouth"* syndrome, the intimate, often sensual sound produced by the individual hand microphone.

Worldly Music Identified

If you combine these into a *"total sound"* —and amplify it to extreme proportions, the produced sound might be called hard rock. Toned down it could be soft rock. Played on an acoustical guitar and sung in a dreamy, sentimental fashion could be folk-rock or blues. But whatever it may be called, whatever its external trappings, the inner character of this music finds its appeal primarily in the physical.

This is the sound of worldly music. And teen-agers love it. This, sadly, is also the sound of much of today's Christian music. And Christian teen-agers love it. It would be a dishonest generality to say that most Christians who perform contemporary music are using these tricks-of-the-trade and worldly styles to deliberately create an earthy effect (though, indeed, this is what is being produced). There are many who are sincere in their desire to communicate with young people. They use the known (pop music) to communicate the unknown (knowledge of Christ). Presenting the unfamiliar by using the familiar as a bridge is a valid teaching principle. But it becomes invalid when a scriptural principle is violated.

13
DISCERNING THE DIFFERENCE

Combining holy words with fleshly music in a song is a scriptural *"contradiction!"* Galatians 5:17 makes this clear.

* * *

When religious words are combined with rock ... the rhythm completely undercuts the lyrics ... the beat making it just another rock song.

* * *

The Rock magazine, Rolling Stone, praised Bob Dylan's 1980 album, *"Slow Train Coming"* as one of his best. The magazine's assessment of the religious content was this: *"The words finally don't matter after all."*

* * *

Christ is the central theme of Christianity. He should also be the theme of Christian songs. It is therefore of paramount importance that the music used to convey the verbal expression of His infinite nature, should be of the highest quality. But today we are busy dressing up Christ in the rags of rock, blues and jazz.

13

DISCERNING THE DIFFERENCE

Scriptural Contradiction

Combining holy words with fleshly music in a song is a scriptural "contradiction!" Galatians 5:17 makes this clear.

> *"For the flesh sets its desire against the Spirit and the Spirit against the flesh; for these are in opposition to one another, so that you may not do the things that you please"* (NASV).

The performer of Now Sound music, whether he realizes it or not, is saying:

Flesh + Spirit = Spirit

The Scripture teaches this:

Flesh + Spirit = Conflict

To try to communicate the gospel using the sensual sounds of the world will only communicate sensuality. This is because pop music has a meaning of its own that overrides the meaning of the words.

Author Jeremy Larner, believing that *"it is the rhythm of rock that carries its psychic message . . ."* relates this incident:

> In a record studio I heard one of the most gifted rock-n-roll songwriters

> recording a trial version of a "pop-gospel" song. As he sang, I became increasingly aware that the subconscious thrust of the rhythm was completely undercutting the conscious intention of the lyrics.[1]

The words were saying one thing, but the music was saying something quite different.

Message And Music Blend

In what seems to be almost an anxiety to reach young people by means of music, many are not only ignoring scriptural commands to the contrary, but are overlooking a basic tenet of communication: the message and the medium must blend together. To be effective they cannot contradict one another. A song, in order to fully relate the intended thought, must wed text and music. This is the principle from which good composers down through the centuries have worked.

If this principle is not followed, wrong interpretations and confusion can result. Then it can become amusing, and may at times border on travesty, as in these two examples:

The song, Love Lifted Me, has long been a favorite of many congregations. The first verse—

> I was sinking deep in sin,
> far from the peaceful shore,
> very deeply stained within,
> sinking to rise no more

is somber. The music, with its lilting 6/8

---

[1]Peck, Op.Cit., p. 114.

Plaguing the Christian retail merchant, also, has been the tightening of credit policies by Word Records since its takeover by the American Broadcasting Co. Word's liberal credit policy in past years has done a great deal to establish some of the larger record retailers. However, since January the tightening of the credit policy by ABC has had rippling effects all across the industry.

Although this tightening of credit will probably be of benefit to the industry as a whole in the years to come, for the stores whose sales are heavily dependent upon albums and tapes this has necessitated some major readjustment.

The overall picture for Christian music today looks bright but tight. Yet there are some disturbing clouds on the horizon. These could bring the blessings of rain or the devastation of hail. One of these clouds is the possible entry of another enormous secular giant, Music Corporation of America, into the religious record field.

To listen to the secular boys talk, they would have you believe that they are really going to put religious music on the map. The smiles on the faces of some of the Christian record producers show that they, too, believe that the Christian music industry is going to be caught up in this whirlwind and swept into new

heights of prominence. It is this writer's belief, however, that if religious music ever gets out of the control of Christians who are ministry oriented, the end result will be just another tower of Babel, with a lot of noise but no substance.

Jim Willems is owner of Maranatha Village in Santa Ana, Calif.

Excerpts from **Contemporary Christian Music,** a monthly publication.

If this principle is not followed, wrong interpretations and confusion can result. Then it can become amusing, and may at times border on travesty.

Like most choral directors, I am always on the lookout for good music to perform. As I was listening one day to a broadcast of the International Choral Competition finals a Hungarian choir sang a beautiful number in their native language. Thinking that it might make a good addition to the next year's repertoire if an English version were available, I ran to get a pencil to write down the title when the choir had finished. After the sublime ending had faded away I waited with my pencil poised for the announcer's voice. Then it came:

"You have just heard [Hungarian Title], the story of the love affair between two vampires." I've never cared much for vampires, so we didn't use it.

Familiar Hymns With Rock Beat

Not so amusing, however, is the great amount of musical trivia in the form of record albums, tapes and sheet music that is today flooding Christian bookstore shelves. It ranges from jazzy accompaniments to children's songs to lavish Hollywood-style orchestrations of hymns to hard rock "Jesus Music." Rivaling the rock version of The Old Rugged Cross as the ultimate in poor taste was a 1978 Christmas album by one of America's leading Christian arrangers. The album included, among other selections of dubious character, a rock beat to Handel's Joy to the World and Hallelujah

Chorus from his Messiah. Even non-believers must cringe when they hear this kind of musical abomination.

When _Amazing Grace_, _O Happy Day_, and _The Lord's Prayer_ were first played on rock stations there was no uprising of condemnation from rock fans. They, in fact, accepted them as theirs, keeping them near the top of the charts for several weeks. Young people were not at all offended by their message. It mattered little what the words were. The beat was there. That's all that counted. Can you imagine the irate calls the local disc jockey would have received if one of these songs had somehow slipped by traditionally sung? Can you imagine any young person, listening to the rock versions of the songs, responding to the message? The music completely counteracts any effect of the words.

The Rock magazine, _Rolling Stone_, praised Bob Dylan's 1980 album, _"Slow Train Coming"_ as one of his best. The magazine's assessment of the _"Problem of Religious Content"_ was this:

The words finally don't matter after all[1]

Christ, The Theme Of Christian Music

Christ is the central theme of Christianity. He should also be the theme of Christian songs. It is therefore of paramount importance that the music used to convey the verbal expression of His infinite nature, and all that is ours in Him, should be of the highest quality.

---

[1]Eternity, January, 1980, p. 55.

But today we are busy dressing up Christ in the rags of rock, blues, and jazz—even presenting Him as a superstar and a clown. Then we tell the world that He is our Savior and coming King—the holy, sovereign God. What must the world think when we, His people, treat Him with such callous disrespect? This is mockery. The church is the bride of Christ. The bride doesn't mock and belittle the bridegroom. The church is to be *"adorned for her husband"* (Revelation 21:2), *"holy and without blemish"* (Ephesians 5:27).

The cry of the times is *"let's be contemporary. Let's have new church music."* Then we proceed to borrow styles that have been the world's exclusive specialty for 75 years. Yes, there is room for new songs and original arrangements. But let's dip into the treasury of traditional musical foundations that stem from the influences of the Reformation. The music that came over on the slave-trader boats doesn't fit our theme.

Musical Guidelines

Whether we are performers or listeners, it is essential that we have some musical guidelines to follow. What should be the determining factors in selecting the music that we perform, the album we purchase or the concert we attend? Because we like the sound? Because some unsaved person might be attracted by it? Because it blesses us? No. None of these are sufficient reasons. We may like the wrong sounds. Amusing the lost is not the function of church music. We may mistake entertainment for blessing.

Key Questions

There are **6** key questions I believe we should ask ourselves concerning our choice of music.

1. Are the words doctrinally correct?
2. Is the message clear?
3. Does the music fit the words?
4. Is it people-oriented or God-oriented?
5. Does it draw attention to the performance (or performer) or to the message?
6. In what way will it edify?

14

FILLING THE VOID

Developing a taste for good music is a matter of exposing ourselves to it. Taste for anything, good or bad, is acquired by what we continually expose ourselves to.

* * *

Philippians 4:8 should be a reminder to Christians that we must reject the junk and develop a taste for the good.

* * *

God intended for us to enjoy music. He put His stamp of approval on it. From Genesis to Revelation there are hundreds of references to music in the Scriptures. Music played an important part in the Hebrew culture. The major portion was used for worship and praise.

* * *

The Christian young person who is caught up in the rock music trap and does not want to change is like the alcoholic who is addicted to the bottle.

14

FILLING THE VOID

A Generation That Knows Nothing Else

Years ago my father ran a small, neighborhood grocery store. Since he didn't drink and didn't think anyone else should either, he carried no stock of beer or wines. One day a customer who obviously had been in the process of depleting his present supply of beverages wandered in and asked for a few bottles of his favorite brew. Dad said that he didn't have any beer but he would gladly sell him some root beer. The gentleman looked at him quizzically and asked, *"What's that?"*

Thousands of young people are in this same sad state musically. This generation knows only rock. To them other music just doesn't exist. When it is suggested that they listen to something more refined like classical music, they might well ask, *"What's that?"* Whether it is secular rock or *"Christian"* rock, this is the only music that they understand; the only music that appeals to them.

The Christian young person who is caught

in this trap and refuses to listen to other music because he doesn't like it or it makes him "nervous" is very much like the alcoholic who is addicted to the bottle. The teenager is actually addicted to the enticing sounds of rock and does not wish to change.

A New Horizon

When the alcoholic is freed from his craving for alcohol, he sees that there is a wonderful world of other things to drink (and better for him too). Likewise, when the young person begins to walk in the Spirit so that he is not fulfilling the desires of the flesh, he is freed from the craving for the world's sensual sounds. The door is then open to explore the other world of music. There is an immense variety of good music to listen to: symphonies, concertos, overtures, marches, sonatas, folk songs, art songs, suites, cantatas, oratorios, semi-classics and many more forms of musical expression.

God intended for us to enjoy music. He put His stamp of approval on it. From Genesis to Revelation there are hundreds of references to music in the Scriptures. Music played an important part in Hebrew culture. The major portion was used for worship and praise. But music was included in other than religious observances. The playing of instruments and singing were sometimes used purely for enjoyment and recreation (Genesis 31:27), in celebration of victories (Exodus 15:1), to accompany festive occasions (I Kings 1:40) and as a refreshing and soothing agent (I Samuel 16:23).

WHAT'S NEW

Resurrection Band
Awaiting Your Reply
Star Song (SSR-0011)

Barry McGuire
Cosmic Cowboy
Sparrow (SPR-1023)

Awaiting Your Reply is somewhat of a milestone in contemporary Christian music as it is the first real "heavy metal" rock album totally produced by Christians. This is the genuine article, not a cheap imitation. It may turn a few heads away and a few radios off, but then this effort is directed at unbelievers. The quality of performance, production and lyrics is first-rate for that audience. The cover art and graphics throughout are outstanding, to say the least. Since this product is destined to receive only limited airplay (because of the musical intensity), Star Song once again proves themselves as a risk-taking company. We say that in the most positive sense.

Dealers: This is probably not the best album for lots of in-store play. Also, the cover might be a little "weird" for some.

Radio: Very contemporary formats only.

This is Barry's third album for Sparrow and easily his best. And that isn't just an idle statement. The songs are the best he's recorded since his *Lighten Up* LP. Barry's voice seems comfortable and confident with the material, and Billy Ray Hearn has out-done himself as a producer.

The title track is an unusual spoken-word song based on a very "spacey" idea...to understand that, you'll just have to hear it. The other tunes range from the very mellow (*Mystery of Life*) to the very rowdy (*Face to Face*).

It sounds as though a lot of time and care was put into this project, and whatever effort involved was well worth it. It's safe to say that this is truly a big step forward for Barry McGuire.

Dealers: Sparrow has big plans and high hopes for this one. *Cosmic Cowboy* tee shirts will soon adorn many bodies, adding impetus to the album's promotion.

Radio: Contemporary and rock formats can play most any cut. M.O.R. formats should stick with *What Good Would It Do, Walkin', My King* and *You An' Me.*

Some of the record reviews that appeared in **Contemporary Christian Music** magazine reflect the approach of contemporary religious music.

**A Taste
For The
Inferior**

Music has been called the universal language. Almost everyone enjoys some type of music. More often than not, in many homes, it is anything but good music. As a nation, believers and non-believers alike, we seem to have developed a taste for the inferior, the trite and the trashy. It blares at us from the T.V., radio, record player and tape deck. It jumps out at us from newspapers and magazines. It even ends up in our breakfast cereal bowl. We are surrounded by junk.

As Christians, young and old, we must reject the junk and develop a taste for the good. Philippians 4:8 is a familiar passage to most of us:

> . . . Whatsoever things are true,
> Whatsoever things are honest,
> Whatsoever things are just,
> Whatsoever things are pure,
> Whatsoever things are lovely,
> Whatsoever things are of good
>   report;
> if there be any virtue, and if there
> be any praise, think on these things.

We probably have no trouble quoting this verse. But do we practice it? **We must.**

Developing a taste for good music is a matter of exposing ourselves to it. Taste for anything, good or bad, is acquired by what we continually expose ourselves to. As an illustration, suppose that a hermit who has lived in a cave most of his life and has been existing on a diet of roots, grubs and squirrel tails, strolls into town one day. Someone befriends him and takes him to a first-class restaurant for dinner. The waitress sets before him a tender T-bone steak, baked potato, tossed salad and green beans. The hermit stares for a moment at the entree before him, shakes his head and says, *"No, thanks, I prefer my own food."*

Now while there may be certain nutritional merits in his root-grub-squirrel tail diet, the hermit would only need to sample the food on his plate to see that this too is good. If he kept sampling the meat and potato meals he would begin to appreciate them more than his former diet. (If you are a hermit and prefer roots and grubs to steak and potatoes please write.)

A Step In The Right Direction

Expose yourself to good ("classical") music. Attend concerts in your area. Begin a tape or record collection. Young people frequently ask, *"Why is classical music so much better than pop music or even contemporary church music? Isn't some of this music bad too?"* That depends upon what is meant by bad music. Modern symphonic compositions with their emphasis on dissonance, poly-rhythms and poly-tonalities (poly meaning <u>many</u>, not a parrot's name) are not *"easy"* on the ears. Because of the nervous tension created by these elements most people have a low tolerance of this type of music. This might be considered *"bad"* music.

From other than strictly musical considerations some classical music might be given the *"bad"* title because of its associations or the composer's intended representation of a particular story. For example, Moussorgsky's A Night on Bald Mountain is all about witches, ghosts and demons. Ravel's Bolero depicts a Spanish dancer whose movements become increasingly frenzied until she ends up in a heap on the floor. Saint-Saens' Dance Macabre has frolicking skeletons.

Three Good Reasons

Aside from these, and a few other compositions of similar nature which would not fit the Philippians 4:8 standard, the vast majority of classical music is worth listening to. Many reasons could be given for this. Here are just **three:**

1. Classical music can calm and soothe, exhilarate, give feelings of joy and contentment—all positive reactions.

2. Unlike popular music (and much of today's Christian music) that has its day then fades into oblivion in a few months or weeks, the music of the great masters, as creative works of art, have stood the test of time. Many compositions are more popular now than when they were written a century or more ago.

3. With few exceptions the foremost composers of the past, whether they were Christians or not, acknowledged a Deity. Many early European composers were influenced by Reformation music styles. Most wrote sacred music. Bach believed that all music should glorify God. Beethoven's personal philosophy was that *"if music does not come from above it cannot reach the soul."*

The following is a list of recordings that should form the basis for any good home collection. Make your choice, then sit back and enjoy. Happy listening!

*Recommended first

Anderson, Leroy
Irish Suite
The Music of LeRoy Anderson

Bach, J. S.
Brandenburg Concertos
Jesu, Joy of Man's Desiring*

Barber, Samuel
Adagio for Strings

Beethoven, Ludwig Von
Symphony No. 5*
Piano Concerto No. 1
Egmont Overture*
Violin Concerto

Berlioz, Hector
Overtures:
Corsaire
Roman Carnival*
Benvenuto Cellini

Bizet, Georges
L'Arlesienne Suites No. 1 & 2*
Symphony in C

Borodin, Alexander
Prince Igor: Polovtsian Dances*
Nocturne for String Orchestra*
Symphony No. 1

Brahms, Johannes
Symphony No. 1
Piano Concerto No. 2
Hungarian Dances
Academic Festival Overture*
Variations of a Theme by Haydn

Britten, Benjamin
Young People's Guide to the Orchestra*

Chabrier, Alexis
Espana Rhapsody*

Chausson, Ernest
Symphony in B^b

Copland, Aaron
Appalachian Spring Suite

Debussy, Claude
Children's Corner Suite
Le Mer
Nocturnes
Prelude to Afternoon of a Faun*

Delibes, Leo
Coppella Suite*

Dohnanyi, Ernst
Variations on a Nursery Song

Dvorak, Antonin
Carnival Overture
Concerto for Cello
Slavonic Dances
Symphony No. 9, "New World"*

Elgar, Sir Edward
Enigma Variations
Pomp and Circumstance Marches*

Enesco, Georges
Roumanian Rhapsody No. 1*

Falla, Manuel De
Nights in the Gardens of Spain
Three Cornered Hat (ballet)

Franck, Cesar
Symphony in D*

Glinka, Mikhail
Russlan and Ludmilla Overture*

Goldmark, Karl
Symphony, "Rustic Wedding"

Gould, Morton
American Salute

Grieg, Edvard
Piano Concerto*
Peer Gynt Suites

Griffes, Charles
The White Peacock (Tone Poem)

Handel, George Frederic
Messiah*
Royal Fireworks Music
Water Music Suite*

Haydn, Franz Joseph
Trumpet Concerto in E♭
Symphonies No. 88, 94, 102

Herold, Louis
Zampa Overture*

Holst, Gustav
The Planets
Suites No. 1 and 2 for band

Humperdinck, Engelbert
Music from Hansel and Gretel

Ibert, Jacques
Divertisement
Ports of Call

Liszt, Franz
Piano Concerto No. 1
Les Preludes*

Massenet, Jules
Le Cid (ballet suite)*

Mendelssohn, Felix
Violin Concerto
Midsummer Night's Dream Music*
Fingal's Cave Overture*
Symphony No. 4

Mozart, Wolfgang
Overture Marriage of Figaro*
Eine Kleine Nachtmusic (strings)
Symphonies No. 35, 40, 41

Mussorgsky, Modest
Pictures at an Exhibition*

Prokofiev, Serge
Classical Symphony
Peter and the Wolf*

Rachmaninoff, Sergei
Piano Concerto No. 2*

Ravel, Maurice
Daphnis and Chloe Suite No. 2
Pavane for a Dead Princess
LaValse

Respighi, Ottorino
Fountains of Rome (tone poem)
Roman Festival (tone poem)
Pines of Rome (tone poem)

Reznicek, Emil
Overture Donna Diana

Rimsky-Korsakov, Nikolai
Capriccio Espagnol
Scheherazade*

Rodrigo, Joaquin
Concerto for 4 Guitars

Rossini, Gioacchino
Overtures:
Barber of Seville*
William Tell*

Saint Saens, Camille
Carnival of Animals*
Symphony No. 1

Schubert, Franz
March Militaires
Overture Rosamunde
Symphony No. 8 "Unfinished"*

Schuman, Robert
Piano Concerto in A
Symphonies No. 1 and 2

Sibelius, Jean
Finlandia*
Swan of Tuonela
Symphony No. 5

Smetana, Bedrich
The Moldau*

Sousa, John Philip
Marches*

Strauss, Johann
Blue Danube Waltz
Die Fledermaus Overture
Tales from Vienna Woods

Strauss, Richard
Death and Transfiguration
Don Juan*
Rosenkavalier, Suite
Till Eulenspiegel

Suppe, Franz Von
Overtures:
Light Cavalry*
Poet and Peasant

Tchaikovsky, Peter
Piano Concerto No. 1*
March Slave
Nutcracker Suite
Overture 1812*
Romeo and Juliet Overture*
Serenade for Strings in C
Swan Lake Ballet
Symphonies No. 4 and 5

Vaughan Williams, Ralph
Fantasia and Greensleeves
Pastoral Symphony

Vivaldi, Antonio
Four Seasons (ballet suite)

Wagner, Richard
Preludes to
Act 1 and 3 of Lohengrin*
Meistersinger Prelude to 3rd Act
Parsifal: Good Friday Music
Tannhauser Overture

Weber, Carl Maria Von
Overtures:
Euryanthe
Der Freischutz
Oberon*

15
AND NOW FOR THIS MESSAGE

There is no difference between preaching false doctrine and singing false doctrine. Yet many evangelical churches are sound in their preaching but allow questionable music to be presented in their services.

* * *

More and more, hymn books of today are omitting many references to the names of Diety in their hymn selections.

* * *

Some well-known Christian song writers are including the sensual rock tunes in their Cantatas, musicals and song books. The words of much of their music are vague at best and the music imitates the world.

* * *

We are producing songs for Christian use that have a message that is watered down, unscriptural and that mixes truth with error. The end result is confusion!

15

AND NOW FOR THIS MESSAGE

**Do We
SING
False
Doctrine?**

Is there a difference between preaching false doctrine and singing false doctrine? Except for the medium of transmission, there is none. Does the evangelical church teach false doctrine? NO. If it did, it would no longer be evangelical. Do pastors in these churches preach the social gospel? Not for long, anyway! Do we sing questionable doctrine in these same churches? Yes. And usually without giving it a second thought.

> . . . *teach us the patience of unanswered prayer.*
>
> *Dear Lord and Father of mankind, forgive our foolish ways.*
>
> *Every promise in the Book is mine . . .*
>
> *. . . The gates were open wide, and all who would might enter and no one was denied.*
>
> *Hark! The herald angels sing . . .*

Does God not answer prayer? Is God the

Father of all mankind? Is every promise in the Bible ours? Does Scripture teach that no one will be denied entrance into the Holy City? Did the angels really sing?

These phrases from familiar songs and hymns may or may not be viewed as heretical. They do, however, illustrate how we can give little thought to the content of our songs, while at the same time we may be doctrinally sound in our preaching and teaching.

Denominational Peculiarities

Though our hymnals do not necessarily abound with false doctrine, there are a few *"great hymns of the faith"* that bear questionable theology. Hymn writers of the past represented many different denominations. Some denominational peculiarities have found their way into modern evangelical hymn books. But these are very few compared to the vast amount of error and confusion that is being published today.

Colossians 3:16 gives us this principle:

> Let the Word of Christ dwell in you richly in all wisdom; teaching and admonishing one another in psalms and hymns and spiritual songs, singing with grace in your hearts to the Lord.

If we seriously consider this text to be the norm—which it is—we would be more careful in choosing our songs. Too often we sing just any hymn or chorus that happens to be on the page that falls open, without giving thought to the accuracy of its message.

**Worldly
Influence**

Contemporary Christian musicians and song writers, like those of the past, are also influenced by denominational ties. But even more, I am afraid, many of them are being influenced by the late 20th century life-style of materialism, commercialism and humanistic philosophy. This is reflected in the lyrics of their songs.

Compare a new songbook with one published 20 or more years ago and you are likely to be startled with the difference. Mostly deleted from many modern songs are the words that charactereized hymns of the past: sin, redemption, salvation, blood, Savior, cross, holy and repentance. They are being replaced more and more with mere allusions to the gospel. Here, for instance, compared on the basis of the number of references to Deity are excerpts from two songbooks published by the same company—one in 1952, the other in 1977

**Song Books
Compared**

Name of Diety	Times 1952	Mentioned 1977
Savior	6	0
Christ	3	0
He, His	11	9
God	6	2
Father	6	2
Jesus	8	2
Lord	2	3
King	2	0
Creator	1	0

The pages of the 1952 publication are filled with words of praise and adoration.

This book dwells on the attributes of the Godhead. The 1977 song book, on the other hand, dwells more on people—our lives, our problems, how we feel. In addition, the message of the modern book is often vague because of the use of the pronouns He, Him, and His without stating clearly who is being referred to. Who is the person "He" mentioned so frequently? In many songs the context does not give a straightforward answer. After reviewing more then 30 of the latest songs, I believe this evaluation could be made for many, if not most of them.

Not
The
Best

Representative of many youth song books published in recent years is <u>Folk Celebration</u> (Singspiration, 1974). Fred Bock, who compiled the songs, writes in the forward the he had chosen *"the best folk tunes, the best tunes from musicals, the best rock tunes, the best tunes that speak scriptural truth, the best tunes that bring someone from the outside to the inside through the claims of Christ in song."*

There are several good songs in the book. Yet there are others, including the sensual rock tunes, that do not measure up as "best" doctrinally. Here are some examples:

<u>Sandals</u> (Wyrtzen)

Verse 1:

> *"The man in sandals came to help the poor and lame,—No one could stay the same after they spoke His name—*

Chorus:

Sandals, sandals, on His feet, dusty roads where people meet. Sandals, sandals came to me, steps that lead past Calvary."

Vague at best. Mostly about sandals.

I've Got Jesus In My Heart (Harris)

Chorus:

"Hear the calling of the dawn, glory, hallelujah I feel it coming on! Lord make me ready for a brand new start—I've got Jesus in my heart."

I feel what coming on? What is the brand new start? Feeling oriented.

Others of this weak theological paste are included, as well as Day by Day from the blasphemous rock opera, Godspell.

The song Unchained Dove by Carol Melton, published by Agape promotes pantheism and liberalism:

"I saw Him in the morning, I saw Him in the dawn. I saw Him in the sunrise and His sunshine lingers on.

"I saw Him in a forest, I saw Him in a tree, I saw Him in all mankind, I see Him in you and me."

And what are the doctrinal implications of this song?

Peace Like a River (Red/Courtney)

"He gives you joy like a soft robe wrapping you up in His love. He gives you strength, like an eagle, hovering high above. He comes hoping to show you the way to be free."

Watered-Down

Hoping to show us the way to be free? Entirely false. . . . Christ came to *"give His life a ransom for many"* (Matthew 20:28).

Unscriptural

Here is part of a Christmas song, Born Again. (Roff)

   . . . *born again, baby Jesus has been born again* . . .

By no stretch of the imagination does this tell scriptural truth.

Mixture Of Truth And Error

Of course, not every song will be a complete theological thesis. But it must include some Bible teaching, and it must be clear. The gospel is meant to be understood. Many of these songs and others like them being published today contain a mixture of truth and error. Should we sing them because they contain some truth? Definitely not. We should reject them because they also contain questionable items and often plain error. Most false religions also have some truth, but these we reject readily.

Folk Musicals Supposed To Evangelize

In the mid 1960's the folk musical, aimed at youth and patterned after Broadway musicals, entered the market. Evangelism was the announced goal. It was thought by the composers that young people would more easily accept the Christian message if it came to them in bright lights, finger-snapping tunes and fast paced action.

The writers of these productions, sincere as they may be, have, like the priests mentioned in Ezekiel 22, made no distinction between the holy and the unholy. Evangelism by way of Broadway will not work.

Paper peace symbols were pinned to mortarboards at Vassar in 1970 graduation ceremony.

From the standpoint of message alone most of these musicals fail to present the gospel in concrete terms. Like the lyrics printed above, the words of the folk musical are often only a potpourri of theological gibberish. The end result is confusion. What is being promoted as truth may be half-truth or even error. The young listener with no Christian background, at whom these musicals are aimed, will not be able to sift out the truth from the error. He surely will get a mixed-up idea of what Christianity is all about.

Tell It Like It Is

William Peterson's enthusiasm for Tell It Like It Is is difficult to understand when its textual content is examined for the evangelistic message that it purports to have. Ralph Carmichael and Kurt Kaiser make this statement in the forward to the musical:

> *The hours of work contained within these pages will only be significant if we hit our intended target—to plaintalk kids into a confrontation experience with the truth about God's love and relationship with His Son.*

There is nothing wrong with their aim. However, in the musical, truth is often evaded or masked in vague terms. In addition to some dialogue there are 21 songs. Included in these songs is enough slang and poor grammar to bring tears to any high school English teacher (gonna, wanna, gotta, comin', . . . etc.) You can read through the entire musical looking for the "plain talk" about God's plan of salvation and not find it. <u>Tell It Like It Is</u> falls short of the composers' target. There is no clear presentation of Scriptural truth—merely hazy hints. There is no mention of our lost condition, repentance or how to make a decision for Christ. Christ is mentioned only three times in the entire musical. Here are two typical phrases from the songs:

> . . . *Perhaps we ought to check Him out more closely. We* $_{(know)}^{think}$ *He is God but what is He to you?* (<u>Know</u> is left optional!)

> *God is interested in you and me wanting us to be the best we can be; we're not perfect living the way we do, but He knows just what we're going through.*

This is not evangelism. This is the social gospel!

Other Musicals Miss The Mark

Other youth musicals show the same tendency toward liberal theology. From <u>Natural High</u> (Carmichael/Kaiser)

> *There once lived a man with a plan that showed us how to live together.*

This could have been Confucius, Karl Marx or an insurance agent. Christ is not mentioned.

From <u>Good News</u> (Oldenburg)

> *We're gonna wake this town and bring the barriers down, and work until the setting sun. We're in a race that must be done, we've heard a challenge from God's own Son.*

From <u>He Is Forever</u> (Nichols)

> . . . *Sin had blinded all their hearts,*
> *so they couldn't share this great love*
> *that Jesus came to share . . .*

Being "*challenged by God's own Son*" and knowing that Jesus came to share His love still misses the mark. True evangelism doesn't beat around the bush. It tells us point-blank what we need to know in order to be saved. These musicals don't do that.

Many more examples might have been cited but these are a cross section of what has been and what is being published. Not all of the new songs and musicals are as off-base as these. However, so many follow the pattern of lyrical ambiguity that this seems to be the rule rather than the exception.

Deceived And Deceiving

These songs and folk musicals are being written by well-known Christians, published by well-known Christian publishing houses and being sung enthusiastically in churches that would not tolerate such mish-mash from the pulpit.

The composers and song writers may have the right motives and the best intentions. But if these examples are typical of their Christian concepts, they are being deceived. And they are passing on the deception to thousands of young people.

Most hymn writers of the past wrote out of a love for the God they knew well. They were men and women with strong convictions, whose songs revealed a more than

"Sometimes I get confused about the impact of a Christian musician in concert," Camp said. "The serious call of Jesus Christ entails extra-severe obedience and commitment. He doesn't want our visibility, but His.

At a recent concert I asked how many people loved Jesus. All 500 raised their hands. Then I asked how many had witnessed about Jesus in the past few weeks. About six to 10 raised their hands. Then I asked how many could explain the Trinity. About three said they could. 'People, you're in love with someone you don't even know!' As His spiritual children we always should be serving Him. But too many of us have forgotten Him; and in doing so, we've laughed in the face of God.

"So it is with this increasing 'popularity' of some Christian artists that bothers me. Hopefully, we can remember it is the greatest servant that is the greatest leader. You don't want people to exalt you, but God. Perhaps these continued days of economic hardship will weed out some of the musicians who are interested only in the financial end.

"It concerns me that in the last few years we've been able to fill the concert halls, but not our churches. And remember, Jesus always retreated from the biggest crowds. I wonder if instead of promoting giant concerts and super TV shows, if Christians shouldn't be urging a return to the prayer closet."

The above excerpts from Bill Cole, vice president of **Light Records,** appeared in January, 1980 *Christian Bookseller.*

elementary knowledge of Scripture. It would be hard to imagine their resorting to some of the sort of Biblical thin-paste or even heresy that we have today.

Money Influences Publishing Companies

Why do men who know the truth promote *"another gospel"* in their songs? A partial answer might be found in a conversation I had with a representative from Word Publishing Co. I was surprised to hear from this man that Word is now owned by the American Broadcasting Company. Did this mean that A.B.C. was setting policy? He assured me that it didn't. The only requisite which A.B.C. had made was that Word make a profit.

Naturally, even a Christian company wants to stay in the black. But when profit becomes the main goal of a business which produces what essentially should implement the Word of God, it is strictly a commercial enterprise. When the pressure is on to make money, the composer, arranger or lyricist will turn to what he knows will sell. Today, that means pseudo-religious words and pop-sounding tunes.

This is not an accusation against the entire Christian recording and publishing industry. Good music is still being produced. But I believe it is only a small percentage of the total yearly output of the combined Christian companies.

If a member of a false cult knocked on your door and offered you some of his free literature, would you take it? Probably not. Would you buy a record, an album of

Christian song "hits" or attend a folk musical espousing false doctrine (but couched in evangelical sounding terms)? You may, unless you exercise careful discernment.

The Great Deceiver

The devil is crafty. He is the Great Deceiver. He knows most Christians would not be taken in by obvious deviations from truth. So he sheds his lion's fur and becomes a dazzling angel of light ... and slips in unrecognized. He doesn't mind a little religiosity. He may even promote some of his own! Just as long as it doesn't lead anyone to salvation in Christ.

As the age of the apostate church nears, Christians need to develop a keen awareness of what is truth and what is not truth. The Word of God is our only guide. We must constantly be searching the Scriptures as did the Bereans, to see *"whether these things are so"* (Acts 17:11).

16

YaBUT...

Some contemporary music leaders attempt to justify their music via Luther and Wesley. They make inaccurate statements as to how the old hymns of the church originated.

* * *

Some justify Gospel Rock saying, *"See how many young people are coming to the Lord as a result of listening to gospel rock."* While this may sound plausible, it is scripturally wrong! God reminds us that obedience is better than sacrifice!

* * *

In rock music ... people respond to the music ... not the message! Such a conversion does not make a dedicated, sacrificial believer ... but rather a candy-coated Christian who cannot stand the tests of adversity.

* * *

The statement, *"You'll never reach unsaved young people with traditional church music"* is not only false and immature, but limits the power of God!

16

Ya BUT . . .

Let's suppose you could project yourself back into the 1800's and hear this imaginary conversation.

Good morning, sir. I am writing a book and would like some information. May I ask you a personal question?

Certainly. Go right ahead.

Thank you. Are you the gentleman who asked the question, "Why should the devil have all the good tunes?"

That's correct.

Ah, then you must be Martin Luther.

No, I'm not. Sorry.

You're not? But many of the recent books and magazine articles quote Martin Luther as saying this. Well, if you're not Martin Luther, then you must be Charles Wesley.

No, sorry again.

Not Mr. Wesley? Isaac Watts maybe?

No.

William Booth?

Nope.

How about D. L. Moody?

Not him either.

Well, I'm confused. In all of my research, this statement has been attributed at one time or another to each one of these men. But if you're not Luther, Wesley, Watts, Booth or Moody, who are you?

I'm the Reverend Rowland Hill.

The Reverend Rowl—? I'm sorry, sir, but I have never even heard of you.

That's not surprising. I'm pretty obscure in the history books compared with those great men. But won't you come in. We'll have some tea, and I'll tell you more about what I said and the issues that were involved at the time. Cream and sugar?

Thank you.

Surrey Chapel Upgraded Its Music

Well, during the time I was pastor of Surrey Chapel in London in the middle 1800's, church music had sunk to a very low ebb. Frankly, the music coming from most churches was very poor. I'm not musical myself, but I believe music has an essential place in the worship service and should be handled in such a way as to honor God. So we upgraded the music in our services—even installed a beautiful organ at a time when organs were looked upon with disdain. And our singing was top quality.

People came from all over London just to hear the music. I believe that church music should be the very best we can produce. Why should Christian music be inferior in quality to the best the world has to offer. Hence the comment about the devil not having all the good tunes. It was in a sermon I preached one Sunday in 1844 that I expressed my opinion on the subject of music. And just for the record, what I said was 'The devil should not have all the best tunes.'[1]

I see. Then your statement wasn't really a rationale for bringing pop music into the church as some have interpreted it, but a plea to put church music on a higher plane.

That's quite correct.

Well, that does clear things up. Thank you so much, Mr. Hill, for your time. I have appreciated this chat. It has been very helpful.

You're welcome. I'm glad I could help.

Arguments Begin With YaBUT

This bit of imaginary dialogue points to the confusion that can arise when we use arguments based on something other than the Word of God to defend our position. Preconceived ideas can always find backing in the vast amount of literature on almost any subject if we are willing to settle for misquotes, erroneous sources or

[1]V.J. Charlesworth, *Rowland Hill* (Hodder and Stoughton, London, 1877), p. 156.

just *"Well, everybody knows that"* information.

Young people especially who have a steady diet of secular rock and want to defend Christian rock will argue when confronted with a passage of Scripture that would oppose their viewpoint. They will brush off the Scripture with a quick, **"Yeah, but . . . ,"** then launch into a well worn argument that side-steps what God says in favor of what man has conceived.

The Historical Argument

These **"Yabuts"** can usually be placed into one of three categories.

Argument No. 1

Some, in error, claim:

> *Luther, Wesley and other hymn writers all used drinking songs as the basis for many of their hymns.*

This argument is a standard *"proof text"* among today's defenders of Christian rock and now sound. While some misuse the statement, 'the devil shouldn't have all the good tunes,' there are others who claim the historical approach as an excuse for using the world's music in the church. Typical is one well-known leader in the "Jesus rock" movement who often cites A Mighty Fortress is Our God and Away in a Manger as examples of drinking tunes borrowed by Luther to set to his hymns. Unfortunately, many young people are making this musician their authority and are being led astray.

These two tunes were never a part of the beer hall life. A look into almost any good

WE
TEND TO LIVE
ON THE
LEVEL OF THE MUSIC
WE LISTEN TO . . .

book on the origins of hymns will reveal the facts.

Luther Composed "A Mighty Fortress"

Luther, being a musician as well as hymn writer, composed the music of A Mighty Fortress himself. Away in a Manger, which sometimes bears the subtitle, Luther's Cradle Hymn, was not written until 300 years **after** Luther's death. Nor was it written in Germany. It came from the United States. According to The Story of Our Hymns (Haeussler, Eden Publishing House, 1952, p. 161) the tune first appeared in a collection, Dainty Songs for Little Lads and Lasses, for use in kindergarten. It was first published in Philadelphia in 1887 by James Murray. Why Murray attached Luther's name to it is not known. He may have used it in order to have the song published more quickly.

Away in a Manger Not Luther's Hymn

This doesn't say much for Mr. Murray's character! At any rate, The Story of Our Hymns ends any debate about the music with this: *"The tune is without question by James Murray."*

The reason for the popularity of the drinking tune theory is not difficult to understand. The implication is that if Luther and other well-known hymn writers used pop music as the basis for hymns then it must be all right for us to do the same. If this were true (and I believe there is no supporting evidence for it), this would still give us no reason to copy them. The basis of our actions must be *"What saith the Lord,"* not *"What doeth people."* When Peter asked, *"Lord, what will this man (John) do?"* Jesus firmly replied, *"What is that to thee, follow thou Me"* (John 21:22). Those words are for us today.

Pop Music Different In Luther's Day

The historical, drinking song argument reveals a basic misunderstanding of popular music as it was during Luther's and Wesley's time. There was no great teenage society that was catered to. There was no great music industry that poured millions of dollars into promotional gimmicks in order to get billions back from these same teen-agers. It was a completely different society from ours. And so was the music. Popular music was just that. It appealed to everyone. If junior sang it, so did grandpa. These were usually simple folk melodies that had been around for many years—sometimes for centuries. They were well-known and enjoyed by the entire family. That's quite different from rock music which is aimed specifically at young people but rejected by the older generation.

The Use Of Common Hymn Tunes

There was also another type of melody popular in Luther's and Wesley's day. In Germany it was the chorale. In England it was known as the hymn tune. These melodies were written in simple meters that could be used in different settings. Most hymn writers, with the exception of Luther, were not musicians. They were poets. They would often write a hymn in a certain meter and set it to a well-known tune with the same meter and that matched the hymn in character and mood. If some of these same tunes were sung in the tavern it doesn't necessarily mean that they originated there. If they had, I'm sure that these godly men would not have used them. Can you imagine Martin Luther stopping by the pub on his way home from work to see if he could pick up any good tunes to go with some new hymns he was composing?

Tunes Sometimes Given Titles

Even today we find many of these same melodies in our hymnals with two or three different sets of words. O For a Thousand Tongues is also O for a Heart to Praise My God. Come Thou Almighty King can be sung as Christ for the World! We Sing. In one hymnal I noted 38 melodies used two to four times as different hymns. The original names of these tunes still often appear in our modern hymnals. You probably have noticed at the top of the page under the main title a smaller name like *Duke Street, Hyfrydol, Regent Square, Redhead,* or *Margaret.*

These sometimes odd titles were given by the composer to identify his tune. The title might be the street on which he lived, an event in church history, his wife's name or even his own.

Since there were in existence a multiplicity of these tunes, the job of writing new hymns was easier for the non musician poet. There was another advantage. Because the melodies were often familiar, a new hymn could be taught in much less time than it would take to learn both the words and the music. This is an advantage appreciated by modern congregations as well as those of centuries past.

There is no question that occasionally one of these tunes could have found its way in-

JIMMY SWAGGART BELIEVES
SOME CONTEMPORARY MUSIC OF SATANIC ORIGIN

Jimmy Swaggart is one of the most well-known evangelists of our day. He is known worldwide not only for his message in word but in song!

Jimmy Swaggart has sold over 8 million records. His crusades are always packed out with 10-15,000 people in attendance. The Jimmy Swaggart Evangelistic Association owns 8 radio stations.

The direction of Contemporary music in the last few years has been of real concern to Jimmy Swaggart. He admits that he was somewhat negligent in writing on the subject of so-called Gospel music and its dangerous trends.

In the July, 1980 edition of **The Evangelist** (Swaggart's monthly publication), appears a 5-page article revealing the sinister seduction of contemporary music. The article, *Contemporary Music*, clearly defines Jimmy Swaggart's frank revelations. He is to be commended for this stand.

Here are some of the excerpts from that article.

> Music, *per se,* has changed somewhat in the last three or four years. Contemporary has become the order of the day on most of your Christian radio stations. Yet, the words have little if any meaning, and the lyrics seem to say nothing. One might compare it to eating cotton candy. It's big, it's flashy, it's palatable; but when it's finished, there has been no nourishment for digestion. . . .

> I feel that this music is wrong; it does not glorify God. In some cases, I would go so far as to say that I believe it is of satanic origin. . . .

> I feel so strongly about this that I have given instructions to the eight radio stations owned and operated by the Jimmy Swaggart Evangelistic Association that they are never to play contemporary music. . . .

> Even though music was originally created in heaven, Satan has endeavored to corrupt, twist, and distort it; as he has everything that God made to be good. Satan has been especially successful in the realm of music. . . .

I am also convinced that the contemporary style music that is becoming predominant in many churches today is not only hurtful, but it is a tremendous hindrance to the body of Christ as a whole. . . .

I maintain that it's impossible to worship God by contemporary music. . . . Contemporary music stifles worship. . . . There's nothing there to worship. . . . The thing is not of God. . . .

One of my radio managers related to me that he was playing contemporary music to appeal to the young people. I relieved him of his responsibilities. I do not feel that you help the cigarette smoker by smoking with him, or benefit the drinker by sharing his bottle. Neither do I feel that you champion the cause of our young people by fostering that which is harmful at the least and satanic at the worst. . . .

There is a horrifying resolve that comes into my heart every time I hear this thing that passes for Christianity. I am disturbed in my soul. . . . Satan is making every effort, with his subtle means, to steal, kill, and destroy. He works within the church just as well as he works outside the church. And many times I feel his subtle advances within the body of Christ cause more problems than that which he does on the outside.

We need more courageous Christian leaders who are willing publicly to take a stand on trends that seek to undermine the ministry of the Gospel.

to the tavern. The same thing can happen today. Before I became a Christian I only knew O Happy Day as How Dry I Am!

However, to equate today's rock music, with all of its heavy syncopated rhythms and dissonant harmonies, with the simple hymn tunes and folk melodies of two or three centuries ago is to stretch the comparison beyond the breaking point.

Wesley and Luther used High-Class Music

Concerning the supposed use of pop music in Wesley's hymns, Eric Routley, noted Hymnologist and authority on the Wesleys writes,

> The Wesley hymns were "pop" only as much as they used music derived from the bourgeois culture of the day, and the upper class culture, rather than the traditional church styles. <u>The poverty-stricken drunks of Redruth and Wednesbury were not providing this music for the Wesleys.</u>[1] (Emphasis mine)

Describing Luther's hymns, Grove's Dictionary of Music and Musicians (Vol. 2, p. 178) reads:

> "Noble words, closely wedded to noble music, severely simple, yet never trivial, these hymns seem an echo of the Reformer's own great spirit. . . ."

Let's let Luther speak for himself:

> These songs were arranged in four parts to give the young—who at any

---

[1]Eric Routeley, *Twentieth Century Church Music* Herbert Jenkens, London, 1964), p. 155.

rate should be trained in music and other fine arts—something to wean them from love ballads and carnal songs and teach them something of value in their place, thus combining the good with the pleasing as is proper for youth. [2]

This doesn't sound like a man who borrowed drinking tunes to make into hymns!

Did Luther and Wesley really use pop music for their hymns? The evidence says no.

The historical argument, then, is invalidated because it is based upon erroneous information, misunderstanding or misapplication of facts.

Gospel Rock Gets "Results"

Argument No. 2

"Look at the results." Or, *"See how many young people are coming to the Lord as the result of listening to gospel rock."*

This is an argument which is not supposed to be questioned. After all, isn't it the results that count? This has a nice ring. But it's the wrong number. For it is the *"end justifies the means"* philosophy. And that is false philosophy.

When Christ sent His disciples on an evangelistic tour of the surrounding countryside He was interested in results. He could have told them to communicate, to relate and not to offend anybody so that people would more readily accept the message. But what did He instruct them?

---

[2]Leupold, U.S., Ed., *Luther's Works: Liturgy and Hymns,* (Fortress Press, 1965) as quoted by Dwight Gustafson, **Should Sacred Music Swing?** *Faith for the Family,* Jan/Feb. 1975, p. 40.

> *Whenever you enter a house, stay there until you leave town. And any place that does not receive you or listen to you, as you go from there, shake the dust from the soles of your feet for a testimony against them (Mark 6:10-11 NASB).*

The disciples were to preach the simple word of salvation. If some would not listen they were not to stop and argue or make the message *"easier,"* but to move on and even testify against their unbelief. Today we will go to almost any lengths to make the gospel more appealing. But God sets the standards. We are to uphold those standards even at the cost of results.

> *And Samuel said,*
> *Hath the Lord as great delight in burnt offerings and sacrifices, as in obeying the voice of the Lord? Behold,* **to obey is better than sacrifice . . .**
>
> (1 Samuel 15:22)

True Results Not Always Visible

Results cannot always be the means of evaluating our efforts. Many missionaries have labored faithfully for years in the field where God has sent them. Yet results in terms of visible signs may be lacking. Moses, too, looked for results when he struck the rock—water for the parched Israelites. But the results Moses received were in disobedience to God's command. God had told Moses to speak to the rock and the water would flow (Numbers 20:11). Moses didn't hesitate. He walked over to the rock and hit it with his rod—twice. He got results. Out gushed the water. But this was in violation of God's command, and because Moses did not follow instructions he was not allowed to enter the Promised Land.

What Kind Of Results?

What kind of results can we expect when we bypass God's commands in favor of our own methods? Here are some that three individuals experienced when they tried the Madison Avenue approach to win teens to Christ.

A former staff member of Youth for Christ in a large metropolitan city sent out several Jesus rock groups to tour the country in the early 70's. Now he states,

> I don't know how much we influenced anybody. It was good entertainment, but not much use in bringing to the kids that the basis of Christianity lies in a commitment to Christ.[1]

One day I talked with a pastor who had been in charge of follow-up after a large city wide evangelistic campaign. Christian rock had been used prominently throughout the meetings. Several hundred young people had responded to the invitation at the close of the services. This is what he reported: "A few weeks after the meetings I had difficulty finding any who had signed decision cards. There were none in the churches, none attending Bible studies, none going on with the Lord at all." He concluded that the young people

---

[1] **"The Jesus Rock Phenomenon,"** St. John's Calgary Report, Feb. 10, 1978, p. 20.

were responding to the music more than to the message. They received a temporary high from the syncopated sound, but when that was gone so was whatever interest there might have been in spiritual things.

A Former Rock Musician's Testimony

Here is the written testimony of Phil, a young man who had been saved out of a rock band:

In 1973 I became a Christian after playing with rock bands and being in the music business for about seven years. I was manager of a record shop and played drums in night clubs and ballrooms. I knew the Lord wanted me to come out from among the crowd I was in, and also that He wanted me to put away the rock music that I loved.

Secular Rock With Christian Words

Some well-meaning Christians encouraged me to "use my talents for the Lord," so we formed a group to play what we considered to be the new Christian sound. It was nothing more than secular rock with Christian words. We thought that the type of music we played, the length of our hair and the way we dressed would more effectively reach these young people. We gave our testimonies with soft, slow music in the background. When we gave the invitation sometimes a hundred or more teenagers would come forward. Were these conversions genuine? We decided to begin a follow-up. We were shocked to find that almost everyone who had given us an address had gone back to their old ways. I can't think of one person I could show you today as fruit of our ministry.

I realize now that they were responding to the music, not to the Holy Spirit.

(Signed) Phil Wilson, June, 1978

Someone may say, *"My friends, George and Betty, got saved at a Christian rock concert."* That may be. But that only shows that the Holy Spirit may work in spite of our disobedience. But what are the implications of this in the lives of George and Betty as new believers? Will they now reject this music because they are new creations in Christ? They may. It is more likely that they will continue to listen to the same music they did before their conversion. Since the contemporary sound is of the world, they will see no need to be separated from the world.

How much better it is to walk in the Spirit, and to live the life that we know, according to God's Word, He can bless.

Thus it is seen that Argument No. 2, *"Look at the results,"* is invalidated because it is based on the premise that the end justifies the means. It doesn't.

Music A Means Of Evangelism?

Argument No. 3
"You'll never reach unsaved young people with traditional church music."

I agree! It is the implied completion of that statement, *"Therefore we must use music they can identify with,"* that causes trouble.

Traditional church music and hymns are not meant for unbelievers.

For the natural man receiveth not the things of the Spirit of God for they are foolishness unto him. Neither can he know them because they are spiritually discerned" (I Corinthians 2:14).

A blind person cannot appreciate a beautiful sunset. Neither can an unbeliever fully comprehend and appreciate music about God, because he is spiritually blind. Once he has experienced the forgiveness of sins, his spiritual eyes are opened and things formerly of little interest now take on new meaning. Only then can the individual know the joy of singing hymns. It becomes a personal expression of worship and praise.

Christian Music A Body Activity

There is little in Scripture to indicate that we are to use music as an outreach to the world. Just the opposite is true. The Bible is filled with references to singing as an exclusive *"body activity"* which is to be directed to the Lord.

Moses and the children sang this song to the Lord.   (Exodus 15:1)

Sing unto Him, sing psalms unto Him.
(I Chronicles 16:9)

As the laying of the temple foundation progressed the priests and Levites

Sang together by courses in praise and giving thanks unto the Lord.
(Ezra 3:11)

The Psalms are saturated with phrases like "Sing unto Him a new song," "Sing unto the Lord," "Sing praises to His name," "Sing unto God."

... and in the New Testament

Singing and making melody in your heart to the Lord. (Ephesians 5:19)

Teaching and admonishing one another in psalms and hymns and spiritual songs, singing with grace in your hearts to the Lord.

(Colossians 3:16)

I will declare thy name unto my brethren, in the midst of the church will I sing praise unto Thee.

(Hebrews 2:12)

The Scriptures teach that the purpose of music is for praise, worship and teaching in the assembly of believers, not to get the attention of unbelievers.

Thus Argument No. 3 is also invalidated because it is at odds with scriptural truth.

Music Is Secondary In Evangelism

Does this mean, then, that there is no place for music in evangelism? No. But it does mean that it can't be used as the carrot on the stick to attract people to Christ. The gospel was never meant to have popular appeal, but to bring conviction of sin and repentance. When we try to sugarcoat this message with questionable music we only show a false picture of the Christian life. The message of salvation is to be communicated by preaching. Music is secondary. When it is used, it should be like giving a personal testimony—proclaiming (through song) who Christ is and what He has done for us. But in doing this we must be careful that the listener is made aware of not only the love of God but also of the cost of being a Christian.

God gave His Son. That was cost. Living the normal (not average) Christian life costs us something, too—a dying of self, being separated unto holiness, being obedient to His Word, having sometimes to stand alone.

Jesus is not some kind of swinging trip. Neither is He a big daddy helper who waits patiently for us to give Him the signal to bail us out of trouble. This must be the impression received by many young people when they hear the gospel communicated through swinging music.

Jesus is Lord. In all that we do we are to worship Him in spirit and in truth. His desire for us is that we be conformed to His image and be holy as He is holy—in music, as well as in all things.

SEQUEL

Early in 1980, in what may prove to be a significant move, several of the big secular recording companies announced the signing of Christian artists to introduce gospel music into the mainstream of the national music scene.

Is this an indication of the moving of the Holy Spirit that will bring the name of Christ into millions of homes by way of recorded music? Or, does it indicate that the final step down in the secularization of contemporary Christian music has begun?

Why would the secular industry be interested in having Christian musicians sing songs about Christ? Why would the world be interested in listening? Is the world going to evangelize the world?

The reason is apparent: <u>Money</u>! Reported in <u>The Music Scene</u> for Jan-Feb 1980 (speaking of the Christian recording industry):

> *Gospel music is a flourishing multi-billion dollar enterprise. Prominent artists can realize more than 75,000 unit sales for a given album.*

It is simply a matter of business. The secular companies are interested only in adding to their profits from what they see is a growing and lucrative market.

Why has popular Christian music become so appealing to the secular market? Does the music provide the answer to spiritual needs, or is it merely another source of entertainment? **Four** factors lead me to believe that entertainment is the primary selling point.

1. Christian music has lost its distinction. Contemporary Christian music has incorporated the world's styles into its own. Today there is no difference in sound.

> Come out from among them and be ye separate. . . .
> (2 Corinthians 6:17)

2. Christian *"pop stars"* move easily from one world to the other. Many of these musicians entertain in night clubs on Saturday night and sing in church on Sunday. Their fans accept them in either place with equal enthusiasm.

> If you were of the world, the world would love his own . . .
> (John 15:19)

3. The gospel has been diluted. Because the message found in many current Christian songs is vague, the gospel is no longer the true gospel and no one is offended. "Gospel" music is now merely a pop style of singing.

> But there were false prophets also among the people, even as there shall be false teachers among you . . .
> (2 Peter 2:1)

4. Commercialization. Christian companies often treat the message of salvation as if it were just another product to be promoted. Such phrases as these abound in the trade journals: "The gospel music industry," "The Jesus music scene," "The Christian market," "The top twenty gospel hits."

> And through covetousness shall they with feigned words make merchandise of you . . .
> (2 Peter 2:3)

The secular companies have taken their cue from their Christian counterparts and have said in effect, *"If they can do it, so can we."*

Bill Cole, vice president of Light Records, weighing the pros and cons of the success of such a move remarked,

> *If for the sake of the world's approval the message is softened; if Jesus' name is omitted lest it offend; then I question whether it should succeed. . . . Someday, Christian artists, executives, or even consumers will be held accountable. . . . Jesus said you cannot serve God and mammon. –*

– Christian Life, Feb. 1980, p. 14.

Christian artists and executives who are looking to a market instead of uncompromisingly proclaiming the gospel of Christ are playing into Satan's hands.

What better scheme could the god of this world devise than to spread a false gospel "of God's smiling approval on everyone"—using Christians to propagate the message through the mass media of music! Because Christian contemporary music so closely resembles the world's own, . . . and because the offense of the cross has been removed from the message, . . . the world will listen. Christians will then be fooled into thinking that they are fulfilling God's Great Commission.

Use this ORDER FORM to order additional copies of

SATAN'S
MUSIC
EXPOSED
by Lowell Hart
with Salem Kirban

You will want to give **SATAN'S MUSIC EXPOSED** to loved ones and friends.

An excellent book to give to those who want to know how contemporary music trends are undermining the Gospel of Jesus Christ!

PRICES

1 copy: $4.95

3 copies: $12 (You save $2.85)
5 copies: $20 (You save $4.74)

- -

ORDER FORM

Salem Kirban, Inc.
Kent Road
Huntingdon Valley, Pennsylvania 19006

Enclosed find $_____ for _____ copies of
SATAN'S MUSIC EXPOSED by Lowell Hart
with Salem Kirban.
***I will pay UPS for small delivery charge.

Name_____
   Mr./Mrs./Miss   (Please PRINT)

Street_____

City_____

State_____Zip Code_____

***If your local Christian bookstore cannot supply you . . . you may order direct. To insure safe arrival, books will be shipped via United Parcel Service. **(1)** You will pay UPS for small delivery charge. **(2)** For actual cost of books, send check direct to:
SALEM KIRBAN, Inc., 2117 Kent Rd., Huntingdon Valley, Pa. 19006 U.S.A.

SECRET ORGANIZATIONS ACTIVE TODAY
invading even the Church
and Sunday School are part of

SATAN'S ANGELS EXPOSED!

by Salem Kirban

ILLUSTRATED

AT LAST! SATAN'S STRATEGY REVEALED!

Most people are unaware that Satan's subtle deception has now infiltrated the Christian church. Many imagine Satan as a grotesque individual with horns. But Satan, who before his fall was an angel of light, now cleverly deceives even those who are born again by his "imitation holiness."

SATAN'S ANGELS EXPOSED reveals how Satan is using an army of Judas Iscariots to undermine believers through "Christian" music, through false healers, through powerful religious groups that reach millions with a polluted, watered-down doctrine.

This "Angel of Light" as the Great Imitator is the "prince of this world" and his successes in the Church and in high political places are exposed ... clearly, concisely. Protect your children and those you love. You need to know the facts!

From Baal worship

To Witchcraft

To Satan worship

And Now Even Infiltrating The Unsuspecting Church!

Satan's Symbols Explained

How to recognize
doctrines of demons!

SPECIAL SECTION Reveals

How secret organizations, whose threads of terror reach back centuries ago, are carefully weaving their power plot to control the world for Satan. Illustrated chapters reveal the behind-the-scenes manipulation of:
The Illuminati, The Golden Dawn, and **Druid Witchcraft.**

Plus! Exposing the strange rise of political and economic power of:
The Bilderbergers, The Trilateral Commission, and the **Bancor Plan** for a universal money system!

SATAN'S ANGELS EXPOSED! $4.95